FROM *the* GROUND UP

FROM *the* GROUND UP

Improving Government Performance With Independent Monitoring Organizations

STEPHEN KOSACK, COURTNEY TOLMIE,
AND CHARLES C. GRIFFIN

RESULTS FOR DEVELOPMENT INSTITUTE

BROOKINGS INSTITUTION PRESS

WASHINGTON, DC

The Transparency and Accountability Project was initiated at the Brookings Institution in collaboration with the Results for Development Institute, where it is now permanently located and known as the Transparency and Accountability Program.

From the Ground Up: Improving Government Performance with Independent Monitoring Organizations may be ordered from:
BROOKINGS INSTITUTION PRESS
c/o HFS, P.O. Box 50370, Baltimore, MD 21211-4370
Tel.: 1-800-537-5487 or 410-516-6956; Fax: 410-516-6998; www.brookings.edu

ISBN: 978-0-8157-0412-6

Library of Congress Cataloging-in-Publication data

Kosack, Stephen.
    From the ground up : improving government performance with independent monitoring organizations / Stephen Kosack, Courtney Tolmie, Charles Griffin.
        p.   cm.
    Includes bibliographical references and index.
    ISBN 978-0-8157-0412-6 (pbk. : alk. paper)
    1. Government accountability—Developing countries. 2. Transparency in government—Developing countries. 3. Civil society—Developing countries. 4. Non-governmental organizations—Developing countries. I. Tolmie, Courtney. II. Griffin, Charles C., 1951–. III. Title.
JF60.K665 2010
352.8'8—dc22   2009049036

Editing and typesetting by Communications Development Incorporated, Washington, DC.

Printed by R.R. Donnelley, Harrisonburg, Virginia.

Contents

Figures

Tables

Preface

Over the last three decades democracy has spread like wildfire across the developing world. Billions of people who once feared to speak their mind now have the franchise and the freedoms of speech and assembly. According to Freedom House's (2008) annual survey of political rights and civil liberties, the number of "free" countries has more than doubled, while the number that are "not free" has fallen by a third. But political freedom is only part of real democracy. Citizens must also take advantage of that freedom by organizing, staying watchful, informing each other, and pressing for change when needed to ensure a government of their choosing that works for them. In short, real democracy requires civil society.

This book is about a small but crucial segment of the civil society of developing countries: groups that we call "independent monitoring organizations." Independent monitoring organizations keep an eye on government spending and service delivery, conducting independent analysis to ensure that the government is acting as it says it is and as its citizens want. Monitoring the structure and use of public budgets is not as dramatic as protesting or running an independent newspaper—but it is every bit as vital to government accountability to citizens. And the existence of organizations willing to engage in the dullness of monitoring public budgets signals democratic maturity. It shows that citizens have grown comfortable with their right to a government that serves them and want to ensure that they have just that.

Civil society organizations often start as advocates for a cause, a sector of government, or a marginalized group and usually have limited skill or interest in the analytical side of policies. But as these organizations mature, many seek a more enduring vision of their role and a more consistent voice in policies, one that will be heard and heeded over the long haul. Because public budgets are the practical manifestation of government strategy and because the resulting programs and services are at the heart of government effectiveness, they become the natural focus of civil society organizations that want to make a difference. Hence the independent monitoring organization.

This book is one of three that emerged from a project based at the Brookings Institution and jointly led by the Results for Development Institute from 2005 through 2009 to support the development of civil society groups, like independent monitoring organizations, that use analytical tools to monitor public expenditures in low- and middle-income countries. The other two volumes are *How to Improve Governance: A Framework for Analysis and Action* (de Ferranti and others 2009), which develops a framework for accountability that explicitly includes civil society organizations like independent monitoring organizations, and *Lives in the Balance: Improving Accountability for Public Spending in Developing Nations* (Griffin and others 2010), which explores what is known about public spending in developing countries and how civil society organizations might improve the situation.

Those books concentrate on the theory and analysis of independent monitoring. But we were not interested in just writing about these ideas. Believing that the best way to learn about monitoring public spending is to start doing it, we devised a competitive small grants program that supported 16 organizations that undertook expenditure- or performance-monitoring projects in health and education beginning in 2007. The results of this grants program were so well done—and covered such a wide range of interesting issues—that we have collected them into this book. This volume illustrates the findings of these 16 independent monitoring organizations as well as—and equally important—the capabilities of the organizations, their processes, and their techniques for using their analysis to influence policies. The Transparency and Accountability Project continues. It is currently working with a new set of 20 independent monitoring organizations whose results will be available in mid-2010. In the meantime this evidence is offered as a testament to the capabilities of developing country civil society in the hope that it offers other civil society organizations a look at the fundamentals—and some of the possibilities—of monitoring government spending and service delivery.

Acknowledgments

This book is a compilation of 19 innovative and illuminating projects. It would not have been possible without the contributions of the talented researchers and communications experts who conducted these studies. We thank each of them for building the foundation of the book and for providing valuable comments on earlier drafts. Their original reports, along with supporting materials, can be downloaded from http://tap. resultsfordevelopment.org/resources, under "IMO Research." The following is a list of the lead researchers, their organizations, and their reports.

Zef Preci and Fatmir Memaj were the lead researchers for the public expenditure tracking study of the health sector in Albania for the 2A Consortium, "Improving Public Expenditure Effectiveness in Health Sector."

Siti Fatimah, Alwin Khafidhoh, and Markus Christian led the project team at the Bandung Institute of Governance Studies measuring the success of national and subnational leaders in Indonesia in reaching targets for education and health spending, "Public Spending for Education and Health at National, West Java Province, and Three Municipalities in West Java (Bandung, Sumedang, and Banjar) over the Past Five Years."

Joseph Asunka and George Ofosu led the team measuring the incidence of and trends in teacher absenteeism in Ghana for the Center for Democratic Development, "Tracking Leakage of Public Resource in Education."

Sharadini Rath and Vinod Vyasulu led the research team at the Centre for Budget and Policy Studies in India comparing education and health spending in two districts in Karnataka, "Expenditure on Education and Health at the Local Level."

Cynthia Brizuela Speratti was the lead researcher for the public expenditure tracking study of primary schools in Paraguay for the Centro de Análisis y Difusión de Economía Paraguaya, "Education Expenditures: Budget Tracking Analysis of Thirty Paraguayan Educational Institutions."

Axel Rivas, Laura Malajovich, and Florencia Mezzadra led the research team at the Centro de Implementación de Políticas Públicas para la Equidad y el Crecimiento investigating the correlation between teacher absenteeism and the economic profiles of districts in Argentina, "Equity and Effectiveness of the Public Expenditure in Schools in Argentina."

Betty Alvarado and Eduardo Morón led the research team studying results-based budgeting in Peru and tracking expenditures in the health sector at the Centro de Investigación de la Universidad del Pacífico, "Hacia un Presupuesto por Resultados: Afianzando la Transparencia y Rendición de Cuentas" and "The Route of Expenditures and Decision Making in the Health Sector in Peru."

Mario Cuevas and Jorge Lavarreda led the research team tracking spending on primary education programs in Guatemala for the El Centro de Investigaciones Económicas Nacionales, "Expenditure Tracking to Improve the Effectiveness of Public Education in Guatemala."

Elzbieta Malinowska-Misiag, Wojciech Misiag, and Marcin Tomalak conducted two studies in Poland investigating health and education financing and the issue of debt in public hospitals for the Gdansk Institute for Market Economics, "Poland: Centralized Financing of Health Care and Education" and "The Use of Public Resources in Hospitals: Case Study of Poland."

S. Sadanand led the team at the Indo-Dutch Project Management Society in India studying health service delivery in Karnataka, "Following the Public Health Delivery Trail."

Igor Munteanu and Angela Munteanu led the research team at the Institute for Development and Social Initiatives tracking education spending in Moldova in the wake of recent decentralization efforts, "Decentralisation of the Education Reform and Spending for Education."

Svetlana Misikhina led the research team at the Institute for Urban Economics reviewing education and health spending at the federal level and in two regions in the Russian Federation, "Public Health and Education Expenditures Analysis in the Russian Federation in 2004–2006."

Lineth Oyugi, Andrew Riechi, Thomas Kibua, Justus Mwanje, and Thomas Muthama designed and implemented two studies in Kenya measuring the efficiency of the secondary education bursary scheme and absenteeism among health workers for the Institute of Policy Analysis and Research, "Expenditure Tracking of Secondary Education Bursary Scheme in Nairobi Province, Kenya" and "Absenteeism of Health Care Workers in Machakos District, Kenya: Incidence, Determinants and Consequences."

Nicholas Adamtey led the research team studying trends in health and education spending in Ghana at the Integrated Social Development Centre, "Review of Trends in Public Spending for Education and Health in Ghana (2002–2006)."

Chitra R. Septyandrica was the lead researcher for the public expenditure tracking study of seven education spending schemes in Indonesia for Pusat Telaah dan Informasi Regional, "Is the Education Budget Efficiently Spent?"

Sorin Ionita and Ciprian Fartusnic were the lead researchers for the public expenditure tracking study of schools in Romania for Societatea Academica din Romania, "Lights and Shadows in the Romanian Schools."

In addition, we would like to thank Erin Beck, Asmita Bhardwaj, Andrea Jones-Rooy, Maria Reyero, and Hannah Stutzman, who produced briefs based on each of the project reports. These briefs are available on the Transparency and Accountability Project website on the same page as the corresponding study.

This book has benefited greatly from the helpful and insightful comments of several peer reviewers of both our initial concept of the book and the full draft, in particular, David de Ferranti, Kai Kaiser, Warren Krafchik, Mary McNeil, Graeme Ramshaw, and Bruce Ross-Larson.

We also thank the team at the Transparency and Accountability Project, who supported the independent monitoring organizations highlighted in these pages and the production of this book: Chinyere Bun, Courtney Heck, Alice Krupit, Graeme Ramshaw, Anna Sant'Anna, and Raymond Struyk. David de Ferranti, Justin Jacinto, Carmen Hamaan, and Anna Sant'Anna helped develop the small grants program.

None of this would have been possible without the support of the William and Flora Hewlett Foundation. Their generous financial assistance was essential—this goes without saying—but the project also benefited from the intellectual engagement, vision, willingness to take informed risks, and the knowledge of this subject area of Smita Singh, Linda Frey, C.R. Hibbs, and Kevin Bohrer, who helped at each step of the process. The Hewlett team was rounded out by Karen Lindblom and Lillian Giraldo, who helped keep the administrative elements on track.

Finally, we are grateful to Lael Brainard, former vice president of the Global Economy and Development Program at the Brookings Institution, as well as her team, for their support.

Improving governance from the ground up

This book is based on a simple idea. No one is better placed to judge a government than those it governs, and no one is better positioned to monitor government services to ensure that they perform well and transparently than the citizens who use those services. This book charts the work of 16 civil society organizations—all from developing and transition economies —that have put this idea into practice. These organizations, referred to here as "independent monitoring organizations," unofficially monitor the decisions and actions of elected officials and unelected bureaucrats. The organizations are small, with limited resources and usually fewer than a dozen analysts. But they have insightfully diagnosed problems with government services as well as offered workable solutions that they have disseminated into the public discourse. And though their results have been out for only a few months at the time of this writing, several have already seen their solutions implemented.

In rich countries independent monitoring is almost a given. Civil society organizations, think tanks, advocacy groups, universities, lobbyists, professional organizations, and the like produce a constant stream of policy analysis, continuously monitor government spending and performance, and regularly offer proposals for change. For all practical purposes, the only outside assessments of rich countries that are done by public organizations are the comparative studies of the Organisation for Economic Co-operation and Development (OECD) and the International Monetary Fund (IMF) Article IV consultations.[1] One OECD government assessing another's education policies and offering advice on how to improve them is nearly unthinkable—though it might be useful in many cases.

In developing and transition economies the situation is the opposite: external assessments of policies, institutions, and expenditures are common—particularly by bilateral donors and international organizations—while those by homegrown institutions are few and far between. The smaller and poorer the country, the less domestic capacity for internal assessment it is likely to have and the more likely that assessments of the government will be external. Because these external assessments are typically connected to aid programs, any policy changes they produce are also heavily influenced by external actors. If assessment from the outside is "external accountability" and assessment from the inside is "internal accountability," one might say that rich countries have less of the former and more of the latter, while poorer countries have the opposite.

The Transparency and Accountability Project shows that external and internal accountability share many features. Indeed, local organizations may take advantage of many of the same tools used by external agents. The key differences are in focus and strategy (see table 1.1, which ignores overlap between the two approaches for the sake of clarity). External accountability is typically achieved through visits of external teams that collaborate with a limited number of consultants from the country. These teams can rarely muster the resources, time, and personnel to penetrate into state and local government activities and may encounter additional barriers, such as language. Thus an external group can focus only on central government policies and budgets. Internal accountability, by contrast, is delivered by local independent monitoring organizations, which range from think tanks to small advocacy organizations. They face the opposite problem. Though usually interested in having a voice in national issues, they tend to approach problems from the ground up and often have limited access to national policymakers. Table 1.1 shows some of the key differences between external and internal accountability actors. The table is far from exhaustive, and its generalizations may not apply to all organizations engaged in either external or internal accountability. But it is helpful for understanding the core strengths and weaknesses of each approach.

External analysts begin their work knowing that the government, their ostensible client, will likely shelve all or most of their analysis and recommendations, unless they carry the promise of new resources. So external analysts' true clients are their own organizations. They conduct analyses to form recommendations that become terms for aid. In the process, external analysts typically produce first-rate analysis and often identify champions of reform within the government to further their cause. But fundamentally, external analysis is for external clients.

Several other characteristics of external accountability decisively influence its products. External analysts, usually professionals, use a standard economic framework to review public expenditures, paying close attention to the macroeconomic

TABLE 1.1

Key differences between external and internal accountability

Focus	External accountability	Internal accountability
Level of government	• National (and large states, as in Brazil or India, for example)	• National, state, and local • Service delivery points
Issues	• Macro framework • External (trade) policies • Growth policies • High-level efficiency and equity • Institutional framework for budget preparation, execution, and fiduciary review • Budget balance and medium-term expenditure framework establishing broad priorities • Poverty profiles based on household data and poverty assessments of program impacts	• Funds reaching the service delivery point • Availability of inputs needed to provide a service • Decisionmaking and budgets: how local needs influence allocations from above • Equity of allocations and allocation formulas across similar locales • Management of funds and services • Monitoring absent employees
Timing of reports	• Driven by the analyst organization; for example, a report on fiduciary systems prior to making a loan.	• Driven by the government's decisionmaking and electoral calendars
Dissemination	• Written and oral dissemination in international language (English, French, Spanish) • Dissemination limited in duration and audience, often private with passive public disclosure	• Written in local or international language or both • Oral dissemination in local language • Wide and repeated dissemination sought through all local outlets
Client	• Self and government (the latter often reluctantly) • Donors	• Citizens of the country, including subgroups • Government and donors (usually for specific projects)
Topics	• Driven by standard economic frameworks (macro, micro, public finance) and assessment tools (incidence analysis, cost effectiveness) • Other special topics of interest to the analyst organization (gender, global public goods)	• Practical problems related to outputs (such as construction), costs and quality (such as procurement), or service delivery • Inequities between groups • Performance • Special topics of interest to the organization

(continued)

TABLE 1.1 (continued)

Key differences between external and internal accountability

Focus	External accountability	Internal accountability
Recommendations	• Broad changes in expenditure priorities, often over multiple budget cycles • Changes in national programs to improve efficiency and equity of spending • Institutional improvements • Procedural, legal, and administrative rule changes	• Specific changes to allocations locally to solve problems (reduce excess teachers to accommodate more nonsalary spending, for example) • Managerial and supervisory changes (to reduce absenteeism, for example) • Changes in amount spent to meet stated governmental goals (for example, if the stated strategy is to raise education spending, then it should rise, not fall)
Monitoring of policy change	• Several times a year over the period of the relevant agreement	• Constant, although attention spans vary and issues change

framework, the revenue side of the budget, and broad spending allocations over time. Thus their recommendations are typically at a fairly high level and would require changes to national programs and priorities. Their reports, in international languages like English, French, or Spanish, have limited and passive dissemination (online and perhaps in a few specialized bookstores). Inasmuch as external organizations monitor the implementation of their recommendations, they do so through periodic, formal supervisory visits, perhaps twice a year, augmented by support on the ground from the organizations' local offices.

By contrast, internal organizations have several clear advantages in increasing government accountability. They can monitor the government 24/7, they work in the local language, and they usually disseminate their findings and recommendations widely and actively to convince their fellow citizens to take action. They also have a personal stake in improving government services. As citizens, internal analysts tend to be problem-focused: something does not work, and they want it fixed. This focus does not preclude the same aims as external agents, but the small organizations discussed here typically know that they have clear advantages in focusing on particular programs or on limited domestic spending issues at the municipal, district, or regional level. Their suggested changes rarely stop with abstract economic principles, although many internal analysts would be perfectly capable of working at that level. Instead, they take much of the environment as unchangeable and zero in on marginal changes that will yield quick improvement. For example, a typical external absenteeism study recommends major reforms, such as changes in civil service rules, improved oversight, and changes to the terms of employment contracts. One Indian independent monitoring organization whose work is highlighted later in this book took a different approach: it started with absenteeism as a given and investigating ways to improve health services while also addressing absenteeism. Another independent monitoring organization in Argentina saw little point in proposing new rules or regulations on absenteeism in the Province of Buenos Aires, as the existing rules were being ignored, so it proposed a set of modest changes that its analysts thought the relevant parties might agree to. While external analysts typically focus on changing the underlying environment, the core concern of independent monitoring is to improve government practices and performance in the short run, given the current constraints under which service delivery occurs.

What is striking about table 1.1 is not that external and internal accountability have different core advantages, but that they almost perfectly complement each other. External analysts offer a kind of accountability that internal analysts do not, and vice versa. The strengths (and implicit weaknesses) of each overlap little. In a perfect world developing and transition economies would all benefit from a balance of external and internal accountability. Each side brings to the table something the other lacks. External analysts often have relatively easy access to data, extensive resources, expertise, and proven analytic techniques as well as the ears of policymakers, while internal analysts bring all the advantages that come with local knowledge: a familiarity with the government and the problems with its services, a focus on making marginal, tangible improvements in government performance, and a facility with the local social, cultural, and political environments that make disseminating results easier and more effective.

Naturally, both sides need to maintain their independence—and the Transparency and Accountability Project took care to ensure that it was not dictating the behavior or compromising the autonomy of the independent monitoring organizations that it assisted. But given these complementarities, internal-external partnerships seem a win-win proposition—and perhaps a promising new way to improve overall accountability of government performance in low- and middle-income countries. This book offers extensive evidence of the benefits of internal accountability and argues for a new partnership between internal and external analysts.

Organization of the book

This book is organized around the process that most of the independent monitoring organizations followed in their work. While producing work of remarkable diversity and creativity, the 16 organizations followed five general steps, each the subject of a chapter. Each step brought new challenges—but also revealed much about independent monitoring and the unique advantages that independent monitoring organizations have in increasing government accountability.

Step 1. Gather the budget data

Regardless of what government service the independent monitoring organization was studying, the first step was to gather information on what the government was spending on that service. In nearly every case, the process of gathering this information was revealing in itself. It required interacting with government agencies and individuals who were not necessarily well disposed to the independent monitoring organization's work. Many independent monitoring organization analysts found ways around this skepticism by developing trusting relationships with appropriate officials and convincing them that identifying areas of improvement for public spending could be helpful for them as well. For many independent monitoring organization analysts this step was also the beginning of a long process of deciphering opaque information, discovering what records actually existed and where, and wrestling incoherent data into a form that could be used to assess government policies and performance.

Step 2. Follow the money

It is tempting to think of following money or other resources as fairly straightforward: money leaves the treasury and is spent on delivering government services. In reality, even government spending ostensibly destined for one program often flows from myriad sources to myriad specific tasks. Construction funding for a health clinic, for example, might come off-budget from a donor, or central government funding for medicine might be sent to a central procurement office, which purchases medicines and sends them to clinics. For many of the independent monitoring organizations, making sense of the complexity of resource flows was a daunting challenge in itself.

Step 3. Examine the spending

After an independent monitoring organization has gathered information on what the government is spending and tracked resources to the level of government services, it can examine whether they are serving citizens efficiently and effectively. This step is the core of an independent monitoring organization's analytical work. Although several independent monitoring organizations used advanced techniques, the most convincing evidence of the gap between government performance and promises or needs often relied on simple descriptive statistics of carefully gathered data.

Step 4. Recommend solutions

Both external and internal analysts typically follow their work with proposals for additional research and recommendations for policy changes. But what distinguishes independent monitoring organizations is that each made a serious commitment to the adoption of their proposals. And thus each made an effort to develop proposals with a realistic chance of being adopted. This goal imposed a unique discipline on the independent monitoring organizations as they developed recommendations, one rarely faced by the typical external analyst, who can generally make utopian proposals without worrying about their practicality or likelihood of adoption.

Step 5. Disseminate and advocate

After identifying shortfalls in government performance and suggesting remedies, the 16 independent monitoring organizations engaged in extensive public dissemination and advocacy of their findings and recommendations. This step highlights some of the organizations' greatest strengths. Many have clearly affected the public discourse, and several have brought about real improvements in government service.

*   *   *

The remaining five chapters use the independent monitoring organizations' experiences and analyses to illustrate each step. Not every independent monitoring organization followed all five steps: some concentrated on what the government was spending, some on how the government was distributing its resources, and some on whether those resources were being used effectively and efficiently. Likewise, not every chapter discusses all the independent monitoring organizations that completed that step. Instead, each chapter focuses on the four to six that best illustrate the step.

The 16 independent monitoring organizations

Who are these independent monitoring organizations? The 16 organizations highlighted in this book represent a new wave of government monitors. They are a diverse group, covering 13 countries in Africa, East and South Asia, Eastern Europe, and Latin America. While traditional civil society organizations conjure images of individuals protesting at government offices, the organizations in these pages categorize themselves far differently—as think tanks, academic research institutions, analytical nongovernmental organizations, and advocacy nongovernmental organizations. Some are headed by former finance and education ministry officials, who have an intimate knowledge of the workings of government agencies;

others are led by long-time frontline service providers or policy activists. Table 1.2 shows some of their characteristics.

Each independent monitoring organization responded to one of three rounds of requests for proposals from the Transparency and Accountability Project and were selected competitively for grants averaging $45,000, along with the support described below. Their analyses, conducted between July 2007 and December 2008, took an average of nine months from launch through initial dissemination and advocacy. Given the limited time frame, each study was designed to be short-term and small-scale; the Transparency and Accountability Project also requested that the studies involve both analysis and advocacy and that they focus on the adequacy, efficiency, management, or fairness of some aspect of social sector public spending. Beyond this, the organizations were free to develop their projects as they saw fit.

Support from the Transparency and Accountability Project

The method behind this small grants program was learning-by-doing. The initial request-for-proposals competition was a way to discover and assist organizations willing to self-select themselves into a rigorous process, one that challenged organizations specializing in advocacy to include expenditure and performance monitoring of health or education in their skill set and that challenged organizations traditionally specializing in analysis to expand into monitoring and advocacy.

The Transparency and Accountability Project was designed to appeal to each organization's strengths by specifying only the broad outlines of the work and leaving subject, process, and methods up to the organization. The project provided only the superstructure: the framework in the request for proposals, the work schedule, technical support through materials and advice as needed, and facilitation of peer reviews for analysts to learn from each other's work. Two meetings were held with all the independent monitoring organization research teams in one place: one to initiate the work and one to conduct a peer review once the organizations completed drafts of their analysis. During these peer-learning events the heterogeneity of the organizations worked to the advantage of all. The sessions were characterized not by experienced independent monitoring organizations teaching inexperienced ones but by a free exchange of knowledge and experiences across all five steps of the process. It was comparative advantage in action: some groups were skilled at analysis, others at finding secondary data, others at collecting primary data, and others at presenting their findings. Because no organization was best at everything, all the groups had substantial opportunities to learn from each other.

These sessions produced tremendous insights into how an external actor such as the Transparency and Accountability Project can help independent monitoring

TABLE 1.2

Independent monitoring organizations supported by the Transparency and Accountability Project

Organization	Country	Year founded	Professional staff	Type of organization
2A Consortium	Albania	1993	5	Think tank
Bandung Institute of Governance Studies	Indonesia	1999	10	Advocacy nongovernmental organization
Center for Democratic Development	Ghana	1998	13	Analytic nongovernmental organization
Centre for Budget and Policy Studies	India	1998	15	Analytic nongovernmental organization
Centro de Análisis y Difusión de la Economía Paraguaya	Paraguay	1990	8	Think tank
Centro de Implementación de Políticas Públicas Para el Equidad y el Crecimiento	Argentina	2000	68	Think tank
Centro de Investigación de la Universidad del Pacífico	Peru	1972	35	Part of academic institution
Centro de Investigaciones Económicas Nacionales	Guatemala	1982	9	Think tank
Gdansk Institute for Market Economics	Poland	1990	62	Think tank
Indo-Dutch Project Management Society	India	1988	11	Other
Institute for Development and Social Initiatives	Moldova	1993	10	Think tank
Institute for Urban Economics	Russian Federation	1995	41	Think tank
Institute of Policy Analysis and Research	Kenya	1994	9	Think tank
Integrated Social Development Centre	Ghana	1987	50	Advocacy nongovernmental organization
Pusat Telaah dan Informasi Regional	Indonesia	1999	12	Advocacy nongovernmental organization
Societatea Academica din Romania	Romania	1996	6	Think tank

organizations overcome some of the many challenges of independent monitoring. The rest of this book focuses exclusively on the work of the independent monitoring organizations. But the rest of this chapter discusses some of the insights that emerged from the collaboration of the independent monitoring organizations with project staff and with each other, on issues from selecting a topic to developing recommendations and advocating for change. These are not intended to be cut-and-dried solutions or blueprints for certain success but simply a record of what the independent monitoring organizations themselves found helpful.

Selecting an analytical topic

Before an independent monitoring organization takes any of the steps described here, its first task is to select a topic. During the pilot phase of the project, differing models of support were tested that provided varying degrees of flexibility in choosing a topic. The first round of grants had few restrictions: an independent monitoring organization simply needed to use public budgets to assemble spending by programs (health and education were the suggested programs) to address a timely and relevant policy question. This request for proposals yielded projects on a wide range of topics: implementation of results-based budgeting reforms in Peru and the Russian Federation; central-to-local government budgeting problems in Indonesia, Poland, and the Russian Federation; and sector-specific budgeting in Ghana and India. These studies were creative and relevant to the local context, but they were so different from each other that opportunities for peer learning across the organizations on analytical techniques were limited—though the organizations still learned a great deal from each other on the policy issues, results, constraints, and differing practices.

Subsequent funding rounds altered the approach, with organizations asked to use a common set of tools—public expenditure tracking surveys and absenteeism studies in health or education—to address an issue of local importance. This approach did not limit independent monitoring organizations' creativity, as this book clearly reveals. The resulting work examined a wide variety of facility types (such as primary health clinics and hospitals), levels of government, and specific programs or funding schemes—but it also facilitated peer review and collaborative skills development. In other words, slightly limiting the independent monitoring organizations' methods enormously improved peer learning while keeping most of the variety in policy issues.

While outside funding can be valuable to independent monitors, independent monitoring organizations must also be able to do work that fits within their organizational goals and capitalizes on their particular strengths—especially with small-scale, short-term projects like those highlighted in this book. Project-specific funding can encourage organizations to stray from their long-term developmental plan. Independent monitoring organizations were therefore actively encouraged to use project funding in ways that would enhance the capabilities of the organizations to achieve their goals both then and in the future. The most successful studies came from organizations that chose their topics in part to facilitate their own development. In some cases organizations achieved this by using a new methodology to study a sector or program that is a focus area for them; in other cases organizations used the opportunity to explore new problems that still contributed to their larger organizational mission. Subsequent requests for proposals have asked applicants to explain how the choice of topic helps the organization develop relative to its strategic goals and mission.

Step 1. Gather the budget data
Budget data are the raw material of independent monitoring. But independent monitoring organizations often face difficulty obtaining data or getting permission to gather data. These barriers cannot be overemphasized, and in most low- and middle-income countries there is an unfinished agenda of transparency that needs to be pursued vigorously. But initial barriers to gathering data are sometimes not as daunting as they may appear. Despite some near-disasters, all the independent monitoring organizations featured in this book solved problems of access to data with a combination of local knowledge and sheer persistence. Formal barriers turned out to be less important than knowing which government offices held the needed data, finding the right people and knowing how to approach them, and working tirelessly to organize information that at first seemed unusable.

This may be an area where collaboration with external researchers might be helpful: external researchers often have the leverage to gain access to information that governments otherwise endeavor to keep inaccessible.

Steps 2 and 3. Follow the money and examine the spending
The studies featured in this book show that most independent monitoring organizations already have or can quickly acquire the skills and knowledge needed to gather primary data and conduct high-quality basic quantitative analyses—tasks that are often integral to steps 2 and 3, following the money and examining the spending. And a little technical assistance can go a long way in helping with these tasks. The Transparency and Accountability Project was designed to provide such assistance to any organization that wanted it. The project set up a help desk that offered independent monitoring organization analysts technical support and that

arranged local mentors who could offer sustained guidance. The project also provided assistance in project planning, background information relevant to selected tasks, and examples of survey instruments to help with following the money and examining the spending. For example, conducting an absenteeism study for the first time is a complex logistical task, so it is helpful to have access to the tools that others have used and to understand the steps involved to allow proper planning. The peer learning and peer review opportunities mentioned above also provided opportunities for professional interaction among the analysts and an opportunity to be a little competitive, as analysts could show each other what they had accomplished. All these elements made a clear difference for the organizations and helped a heterogeneous group produce impressive results in a limited time frame.

Step 4. Recommend solutions

Independent monitoring organizations have clear advantages in developing recommendations, and those featured in this book proved masters at the particulars of local decisionmaking and "the art of the possible." Several of their recommendations were so clever and obvious that it seems a given that they should be implemented immediately. But designing feasible recommendations presented challenges for some organizations, some of which the peer review process helped address. Sometimes recommendations that could solve a problem would contravene the purpose of the policy being studied. For example, per student financing of primary schools is unfair to small schools, and an independent monitoring organization studying equity in education funding might advocate doing away with it. But per student financing aims to make funding transparent and equal for each child and to encourage the consolidation of schools so small that one teacher teaches several grades. Given these policy goals, an organization arguing for higher funding for smaller schools might not get far. The peer review process allowed independent monitoring organizations' recommendations to be discussed among an international audience of different perspectives and backgrounds, helping organizations pare down recommendations, eliminate unrealistic or misdirected recommendations, and concentrate on the recommendations most likely to produce tangible improvements in government services.

Step 5. Disseminate and advocate

The independent monitoring organizations needed little or no support on dissemination and advocacy. These are areas where external monitors have the most trouble, but they are the bread and butter of the sort of organizations participating in the Transparency and Accountability Project. The 16 independent monitoring organizations that participated in the project knew their target audiences and developed innovative ways to reach them—from videos to cartoons to press conferences to providing content for other advocacy organizations that could push the recommendations as their own, all in local languages and appropriate to local audiences. The independent monitoring organizations' target audiences were frequently government officials, but some of the most effective and useful recommendations and dissemination and advocacy strategies were directed toward service users and other nongovernmental organizations. Many analysts appeared on television or radio as they pressed their findings and recommendations. And peer learning events provided a forum for independent monitoring organizations not only to share milestones and successful dissemination products with their peers but also to compare advocacy strategies and ideas with like-minded organizations. In follow-up conversations after the project, independent monitoring organization representatives frequently cited fellow grantees' methods and tools as new strategies for their organization to test. Even now, just months after the conclusion of the first phase of the Transparency and Accountability Project, the effectiveness of these efforts in learning and impact on the ground is easily apparent. The following pages show that many of the independent monitoring organizations' findings and recommendations are now fully integrated into the public discourse of their countries, and in several cases, already adopted.

What cannot be done locally is international dissemination of these independent monitoring organizations' work—to other independent monitoring organizations that could undertake similar work in their own locales and to external monitors that might not realize the opportunities they are missing. That dissemination is our responsibility, and this book is part of that effort.

Note

1. An obligation of IMF membership, Article IV consultations are typically an annual independent external review and assessment by IMF staff of a country's economic performance and policies, the results of which are discussed by the IMF's Executive Board.

Gather the budget data

To determine the effectiveness of government spending, independent monitoring organizations first need information on government spending, including what the government is spending and how the amounts are decided and allocated. Gathering this information is seldom simple. Many central governments make available budget data that are too aggregated to tell where each peso or rupee was allocated. The officials who handle the money may not need or want good records of how much comes in and goes out, from where and to what. Even where good information exists, it may not be accessible. It may be buried in a ministry archive, guarded by bureaucratic apathy. It may be scattered in hundreds of local government offices, schools, or clinics and produced by instinct and custom rather than the parsimonious templates of accounting, economics, or public administration. It may be available only for some districts or some activities—the amount spent on teacher salaries but not on textbooks, for example. And analysts may have no right to it. Many developing countries lack a freedom of information act, and those that have one can still protect their information with endless forms, fees, and bureaucratic delay. A large international donor, offering millions in aid, may prevail on a government to provide information and bring in technical experts to crunch the numbers into something useable. But what can a small independent monitoring organization do?

A lot, actually. Independent monitoring organizations have substantial advantages in gathering budget information. The first is their size: there is little chance that a small independent monitoring organization will turn a threatening international spotlight on government underperformance, as external monitors can. Independent monitoring organizations also have an intuitive sense of what data they need. They have a lifetime of living with the government, know how it operates, and thus have a good sense of which data will reveal what the government is doing with its money. They may even know civil servants or other civil society organizations with access to the data. They can then review the data already knowing how the system works and identify gaps and what seems right and wrong.

The message of this chapter is that these advantages are not merely theoretical. The independent monitoring organizations supported by the Transparency and Account- ability Project realized them. The five organizations highlighted in this chapter reveal the opaque process through which their taxes are spent and then clarify it. One dem- onstrates how independent monitoring organization analysts can acquire budgetary information even without a freedom of information act. Another shows how analysts can identify the tendencies of a budgeting process to allocate money inefficiently, even when that budgeting process seems impenetrably complex. The third uncovered the roles and responsibilities of various levels of government in the budgeting process, even when the officials themselves did not understand it. The fourth found a disturb- ing disconnect between government rhetoric and performance hidden in the opaque budgets of two districts. And the fifth painstakingly documented budgetary evidence of government priorities despite operating in a challenging environment.

Integrated Social Development Centre, Ghana

Independent monitoring organizations may begin their analysis without the legal right to the information they need. But the Integrated Social Development Centre (ISODEC), a Ghanaian independent monitoring organization, illustrates the value of trying anyway.[1] Ghana is one of many developing countries that lack a freedom of information act (though one is awaiting parliamentary approval). But ISODEC found ways around this legal impediment to show that it is possible for Ghanaian citizens to gather information about their government's spending. ISODEC's data gathering also revealed the incompleteness of available information and other seri- ous problems with Ghanaian budgeting.

ISODEC's strategy might be called "creative persistence." Analysts set out to examine local and regional budgeting for health and education in Ghana. Before beginning, they smoothed their path by gaining approval from the head office of the relevant central government ministries—approval indispensible for getting regional and district authorities to cooperate. But approval was hardly sufficient: many regional and district authorities were still hesitant to give out information. Requests for budget and spending records were often answered only after substan- tial delays, after analysts were repeatedly requested to come back later.

ISODEC analysts discovered one reason for this hesitancy when they eventually received the records: the information was sometimes incomplete or inaccurate. It was often impossible for analysts to compare spending across districts. Education and health policymaking in Ghana is largely top-down—set nationally and followed by regional and district governments—and most resources come from the central government, with some additional resources from donors. ISODEC analysts measured the share of resources actually disbursed as a percentage of planned spending for both education and health. They gathered 2002–06 spending data on health for 3 of 10 regions—Northern, Upper West, and Western (table 2.1)—and on education for 3 regions—Brong Ahafo, Northern, and Upper West (table 2.2). The data show that regions do not always receive what they are promised; in many cases they receive less; in a few cases, more.

Data vary widely from year to year, but the figures from the Upper West Region are remarkably stable, suggesting that regional records are simply copied from records provided to regional and district departments from central government ministries. For citizens who want to know whether their district is getting its fair share of government spending, these are disturbing findings.

ISODEC's effort to unearth budget information also yielded insights into how different levels of the Ghanaian government communicate and coordinate their activities. The short version is that they do not. Through focus group discussions and interviews with government officials, ISODEC discovered a worrying dearth of information sharing about education and health budgeting, especially at the local level. First, information seems not to be shared vertically. Lower levels of government do not seem to be accountable for implementing promised policies or

TABLE 2.1

Actual expenditure as a share of planned expenditure for health in three regions of Ghana, 2002–06 (percent)

Year	Northern Region		Upper West Region		Western Region	
------	Central government	Donor	Central government	Donor	Central government	Donor
2002	—	—	100.4	—	93.7	81.5
2003	86.2	84.7	78.9	—	66.3	101.4
2004	62.8	65.7	83.8	115.2	72.9	358.7
2005	87.5	109.6	57.8	88.9	77.6	144.9
2006	86.0	34.0	29.1	41.4	85.2	78.7

— is not available.

Source: Adamtey and others 2007.

TABLE 2.2

Actual expenditure as share of planned expenditure for education in three regions of Ghana, 2002–06

| Year | Brong Ahafo Region | | Northern Region | | Upper West Region | |
	Central government	Donor	Central government	Donor	Central government	Donor
2002	1.7	14.6	528.1	—	66.7	100.0
2003	6.0	—	200.8	—	66.7	100.0
2004	123.5	88.6	200.7	100	66.7	100.0
2005	21.8	31.1	186.1	100	66.7	58.9
2006	64.9	—	119.9	100	77.7	100.0

— is not available.

Source: Adamtey and others 2007.

for allocating funds as suggested by the central government. Second, government departments in the same area often fail to communicate. District-level departments, for example, rarely know where their money comes from or what other districts are spending. In one district that ISODEC analysts visited, education officials did not even know what their district assembly had spent on education. These local officials miss the opportunity to coordinate their activities and learn from each other's successes and failures, possibly leading to misallocated resources and repeated implementation of flawed policies.

ISODEC lays the blame in part on an inert civil society. Grassroots civil society organizations rarely do what ISODEC did: monitor local service budgeting. Nor do they try to increase awareness of budgeting problems or advocate for improvements. Naturally, civil society is hampered by the same lack of transparency that made ISODEC's analysis difficult. But ISODEC also argues that part of the impetus is on civil society to pay more attention to how resources for local services are provided and used. If grassroots civil society organizations increased the attention on and monitoring of service delivery, government officials might gradually feel the need to improve their recordkeeping—which in turn would make grassroots monitoring easier. ISODEC's analysis shows that such monitoring is possible and useful, and its example should help lead the way.

El Centro de Investigación de la Universidad del Pacífico, Peru

Budgeting transparency in Peru is thwarted by another demon—complexity. The Research Center of the University of the Pacific (Centro de Investigación de la Universidad del Pacífico, CIUP), a Peruvian independent monitoring organization, wanted to investigate the budgetary bottlenecks to increasing access to public healthcare.[2] But tackling this issue threw CIUP's analysts into the maze of Peruvian budgeting, a process so complex that spending seems nearly impossible to trace. After painstaking examination they were able to trace the flow of healthcare money. They then discovered two problems with the budgeting process that undermined the quality of healthcare: the flow of funds from the budget to health facilities was interrupted by myriad bottlenecks and the health facilities themselves have almost no control over their spending.

CIUP focused on two programs—the National Health Strategy for Immunization and the National Health Strategy for the Prevention and Control of Tuberculosis. Because these two programs are national priorities, analysts reasoned that they would have fewer bottlenecks than the average healthcare program would. They began by tracing the flow of money for the two programs into 14 health centers in one of the five areas of Metropolitan Lima. Their findings are shown in figure 2.1.

Figure 2.1 is a maze of complexity. But CIUP analysts, drawing on their local knowledge, reconstructed it in less than a month—in large part because one of the lead analysts had previously worked on the financing side of a Peruvian health project and therefore had some knowledge of the system. Because of her expertise, CIUP did not have to spend all its time trying to make sense of the flows and could instead try to understand the problems with each flow.

Peru's budgeting process is structured around two types of institutions: budget units and expenditure units. Budget units are umbrella institutions and national programs to which money is allocated; in health, for example, there is the Ministry of Health and the National Health Insurance System (Seguro Integral de Salud). Below them are expenditure units, which can allocate and spend. There are two expenditure units relevant to the programs that CIUP investigated: the health directorates and the health networks. CIUP's analysis focused on the Barranco-Chorrillos-Surco Network in South Lima, the second of five health directorates in Metropolitan Lima. The 14 health facilities selected from this network are not expenditure units, meaning that they have very little control over their spending. Most major expenditure decisions are made by the expenditure units and budget units that oversee the health facilities. The only monetary discretion that health facilities have is a small petty cash fund.

That is the structure of funding after it is allocated. But in tracing funding for the immunizations and tuberculosis programs, CIUP found an additional layer of complexity: funding does not all come from one place. Funding for the immunizations program comes largely from the national treasury (70 percent), with additional funding from donations and refundable external resources or loans (15

FIGURE 2.1

Map of resource flows to healthcare facilities in Peru

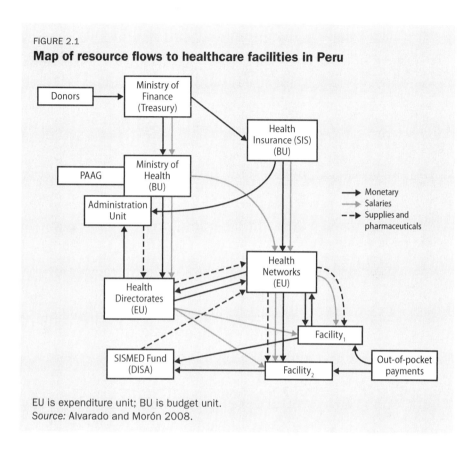

EU is expenditure unit; BU is budget unit.
Source: Alvarado and Morón 2008.

percent) and other sources (15 percent), including the private sector. Funding for the tuberculosis program is more difficult to track, because it is still considered a strategy rather than a program; as a result, funding comes from a multitude of budget units.

This complexity leads to a nontransparent web of funding streams and conceals several problems. One is a near lack of control by the health facilities over their own spending. Others include bottlenecks that undermine the effectiveness of spending and diminish accountability (see chapter 3).

Bandung Institute of Governance Studies, Indonesia

A third barrier to transparency is ignorance. When the Bandung Institute of Governance Studies (BIGS) in Indonesia tried to gather budget data, it found that lower levels of government are not always aware of what they should be doing.[3]

Indonesia recently became one of the world's most decentralized countries. In 2001, three years after the resignation of Soeharto, the longtime Indonesian president, a new law gave local governments the power to run many programs as they see fit. Tremendous optimism accompanied the decentralization, which was perceived as a way of improving government service delivery by empowering those closest to people's needs.

BIGS wanted to examine how well local governments are delivering health and education services. Analysts gathered spending and performance data at the national level and in three cities in the province of West Java: Bandung, a sprawling city with a large budget but a recent history of very poor service delivery; Banjar, a city with a particularly active and responsive mayor; and Sumedang, where civil society and nongovernmental organizations have a strong presence in both advocacy and service delivery.[4]

But as analysts began gathering information, they quickly discovered that the rapid decentralization had left local governments scrambling to understand their new responsibilities. Officials, especially at the lowest levels, expressed uncertainty about what they need to do and whom they answer to. For example, city government officials reported the impression that the national government manages infrastructure for education, the provincial government manages teacher capacity development, and they implement predesigned programs—but budget records do not show this division of labor. Disputes frequently arise between levels of government over authority—including disagreements over who has the final word. Such misunderstandings naturally lead to inefficiency: redundancies in some areas and neglect in others.

This inefficiency is especially worrying because governments at all levels are not allocating as much money to health and education as they are legally obliged. Improving health and education was a particular motivation of the decentralization, and the national government mandated proportions of both national and local budgets for the two sectors—15 percent of the budget must go toward health and 20 percent toward education. The national government does not meet its requirement, but it was hoped that local governments would do better. BIGS analysts, after collecting mostly unpublished budget data, found that some do and some do not.[5]

On health spending, only Banjar comes close to the national 15 percent requirement: 11.4 percent of city spending in 2004 rising to 13.4 percent in 2006—though it fell to 9.7 percent in 2007. Sumedang spent less—between 10.3 percent in 2004 and 7.7 percent in 2006—and Bandung even less—4.4 percent in 2004 and 6.1 percent in 2006. Even this was higher than the West Java provincial government's spending, which averaged 1.9 percent over 2004–07, and the national government's spending, which averaged 1.8 percent.

The three city governments were closer to meeting the national education requirement of 20 percent. Bandung exceeded the mark, spending almost 30 percent of its budget on education from 2005 to 2007.[6] Sumedang's education spending fluctuated wildly, from 8.7 percent of the budget in 2005 to 25.6 percent in 2006 and 5.6 percent in 2007. Banjar, which performed best in health, had the lowest spending on education.[7] As with health, city governments were closer to meeting the budget education standards than both the provincial and national governments were. The West Java provincial government allocated only 4 percent of its budget to education in 2005. The national government spent 4 percent of its budget on education in 2003 and 7.1 percent in 2007.

The inevitable conclusion is that Indonesian decentralization did not deserve the blanket optimism that accompanied it. Not only are local officials confused and uninformed about their new responsibilities, leading to needless inefficiency, but local governments vary widely in meeting spending targets. Decentralization may have created some service delivery improvement but not in all districts.

Centre for Budget and Policy Studies, India

The mere act of gathering budget data can sometimes reveal gaps between a government's promises and its performance. The Centre for Budget and Policy Studies (CBPS) found this in the Indian state of Karnataka.[8] The government there has substantially decreased its real spending on health and education since 2001, despite a growing budget and promises that it was making health and education a priority.

In Karnataka, state transfers provide all district-level funding for health and education. CBPS's original plan was to examine whether these state transfers varied according to district needs. CBPS began by reviewing spending on health and education in two districts of the state, Chitradurga and Udupi, both of which have more than a million people. Each district has an elected council, but it has almost no voice in requesting funds from the state or in deciding how to spend them. Teachers and medical personnel are posted by the state government. Chitradurga is substantially worse off than Udupi on every socioeconomic indicator, so CBPS's hypothesis was that Chitradurga would receive a higher allocation of funds. That seemed a simple notion to test, but CBPS analysts were stunned by what they uncovered.

First, it was almost impossible to figure out how money was spent on health and education because of the mind-numbing detail in the budgets. Education is financed through a budget that has 60 line items determined at the state level—there are multiple lines for toilets and blackboards and three separate lines for scholarships. Only by sitting with accountants could analysts start to classify expenditures for primary and secondary schools, for capital and recurrent costs, and for wages and other items. Health spending was equally opaque; its budget had 58 line items.

Once CBPS analysts organized the numbers into something usable, they were finally able to test their hypothesis that more funds would go to the district with poorer human development indicators. But the hypothesis was wrong: the state did not allocate more funding to Chitradurga, the district with substantially poorer literacy and health conditions. They also found that salaries squeezed out all other inputs, making the delivery of high quality services difficult.

But CBPS analysts also found something totally unexpected: real expenditures had been dropping since 2001 on both health and education. This was a period of fast growth in the state economy, and one during which the state government had publicly committed to improving health and education.

Perhaps there is no clearer example among the independent monitoring organizations featured in this book of a situation where simply gathering the data had such an impact on the analysts. CBPS analysts were so surprised by their findings that they decided to look at expenditures at the state level and discovered that Chitradurga and Udupi were not unique cases.[9] In real terms expenditure on health at the state level dropped 13 percent between 2001 and 2004 and recovered only partially by 2006. Education expenditures did better, dropping 4 percent from 2001 to 2004 and more than fully recovering by 2006. But CBPS also found that during this period state revenues grew almost three times faster than education expenditures and almost five times faster than health expenditures. In other words, the money was there, but it was allocated to other priorities, despite the government's promises. For example, the government promised to shrink subsidies to power companies, but power subsidies grew faster than state revenue over the period. The strategy apparent in the numbers was clearly not the strategy in politicians' speeches. In recent months CBPS forced this issue at the highest levels and made it the centerpiece of its 10th anniversary activities.

Institute for Urban Economics, Russian Federation

Like CBPS, the final independent monitoring organization in this chapter, Moscow's Institute for Urban Economics (IUE), uncovered important information about government priorities in the course of gathering data on government spending.[10] IUE gathered data on central and regional government budgets for health and education in two of the Russian Federation's 83 regions, Chuvash Republic and Kaliningrad. The central Russian government has traditionally depended on regional governments to fund social services, which often left poorer regions with inadequate resources for healthcare and education. But IUE found that the Chuvash Republic, the poorer of the two regions, funds health and education more effectively and innovatively.

The Chuvash Republic is in the center of the European Russian Federation on the Volga River and had about 1.3 million people and a GDP per capita of $1,852 in 2007, less than a third of Kaliningrad's $6,058. Kaliningrad is a Russian exclave on the Baltic Sea between Poland and Lithuania and had a population of less than a million in 2007. Although the Chuvash Republic has lower income and more poor citizens (26 percent in 2006 compared with Kaliningrad's 20 percent), it has been at the forefront of health and education reforms in the Russian Federation and was one of three Russian regions to participate in a program to improve the cost-effectiveness of its spending and reorient public budgeting to objectives instead of inputs.

Assembling the spending data was far from trivial. IUE's effort was successful largely because of its previous work in the two regions and its reputation as a responsible analytical organization, a reputation used to gain access to data that might otherwise be hard to come by. IUE analysts first needed basic information on federal government spending, on spending in the two regions, and on the distribution of spending in the two regions between the federal and regional governments. Rapid growth in the Russian economy allowed spending on healthcare to surge. Spending on health increased from 7.9 percent of all government spending in 2004 (federal plus regional and local) to 10.2 percent in 2006 (table 2.3). Of this, the federal budget contributed 23 percent (1.8 percent of its budget) in 2004 and 33 percent (3.4 percent of its budget) in 2006, a real increase of 73 percent. In the Chuvash Republic real spending on health increased 66 percent over 2004–06; by 2006 the regional government devoted 19.8 percent of its budget to health. In Kaliningrad real spending on health rose 65 percent. But because the regional Kaliningrad government's budget grew faster and because it had spent less on healthcare, by 2006 Kaliningrad's government was spending only 13.6 percent of its budget on healthcare, far less than what the Chuvash Republic's government was spending.

By 2006 the Chuvash Republic and Kaliningrad were spending roughly the same amount per capita on health, about RUB 3,000, despite Kaliningrad having triple the per capita GDP of the Chuvash Republic. In both regions much of the spending was by local governments: in the Chuvash Republic municipal governments accounted for 45 percent of the total; in Kaliningrad, 37 percent. In short, IUE shows that health spending is largely a regional phenomenon with a large

TABLE 2.3

Government spending on health and education in the Russian Federation, Chuvash Republic, and Kaliningrad Region, 2004–06

Indicators	2004		2005		2006	
	Millions of 2004 rubles	Share of total (%)	Millions of 2004 rubles	Share of total (%)	Millions of 2004 rubles	Share of total (%)
Russian Federation, consolidated						
Health	—	7.9	—	9.3	—	10.2
Education	—	12.7	—	13.2	—	14.0
Russian Federation, federal						
Health	—	1.8	—	2.5	—	3.4
Education	—	4.5	—	4.6	—	5.0
Chuvash Republic						
Health	2,073.5	15.7	2,632.3	16.8	3,894.8	19.8
Education	2,971.6	22.6	3517.4	23.7	4,165.3	24.0
Kaliningrad						
Health	1,486.0	13.0	1,997.1	14.2	2,458.1	13.6
Education	2,595.7	22.7	3,194.6	22.7	4,821.5	26.6

— is not available.

Source: Institute for Urban Economics 2007.

municipal component, that the fiscal effort therefore depends on regional priorities, and that spending at every level increased during this short and prosperous period, with the federal government assuming a larger role.

IUE then dug deeper into these spending figures to see how spending differs between the regions and how each interacts with federal programs and priorities. They found two main similarities. In both Chuvash Republic and Kaliningrad capital spending for health increased from 2004 to 22 percent of the total in 2006—consistent with the federal priority to support upgrading the long-neglected physical plant and equipment in the health sector. Both have also increased the share of spending for medical services that are financed by the health insurance fund—consistent with a federal priority to shift medical care funding to a single source.

But the two regions differ in all other aspects. The Chuvash Republic has prioritized sport and physical culture to encourage healthy lifestyles, which is a strategy to address the Russian Federation's high adult morbidity and mortality rates. These expenditures now account for over 10 percent of its health spending, compared with 5 percent of Kaliningrad's health spending. The Chuvash Republic has also been more successful in shifting spending priorities from inpatient care to outpatient and day surgery care, although it still has a long way to go to reach international standards in these areas. Perhaps most clearly, though, because of an early start in reforming its healthcare system to develop primary care as the entry point for the population, it now has 2 general medical doctors per 10,000 people, compared with only 0.2 in Kaliningrad and 1.0 in Russia as a whole.

The Chuvash Republic's efforts are consistent with federal programs to promote healthy lifestyles, reduce dependence on hospitals, deploy primary healthcare physicians as the core component of health delivery (a sharp break from the Soviet model), and narrow budget flows for medical care to a single channel to improve transparency. IUE analysts concluded that the Chuvash Republic's success was due to its early efforts to reform and implement "budgeting by objective": by 2006 more than 24 percent of the Chuvash Republic's budgeting was program based, compared with 9 percent at the federal level and only 6 percent in Kaliningrad. IUE also points out that many of the reforms now supported at the federal level were pioneered in just a handful of reform-minded regions, including Chuvash Republic.

IUE also undertook an exhaustive analysis of education spending in the two regions, of which a few highlights are presented here. The education data tell a somewhat different story than the health data (see table 2.3). Overall spending as a proportion of public budgets is higher for education—14 percent in 2006—than for healthcare. The absolute amount of federal education spending rose 48 percent in real terms over 2004–06, but this was due to growth in the volume of federal spending—education's share of total federal spending rose only from 4.5 percent to 5.0 percent.

In 2006 the federal government financed about 36 percent of the country's total spending on education, but this spending was almost exclusively for vocational and higher education, with general primary and secondary education the responsibility of local governments. Data for the Chuvash Republic and Kaliningrad suggest that both dedicate nearly a quarter of spending to education. However, local governments—not the region—provide nearly 80 percent of funding for preschool, general primary, and general secondary education. (In both regions there is virtually no spending on higher education because it is the federal government's responsibility.) Prior to 2006 Kaliningrad lagged behind the Chuvash Republic in total spending on education, but a surge in 2006 moved it well ahead, in large part because of new capital spending. In 2006 Kalinigrad spent RUB 5,565 per capita, 60 percent more than the Chuvash Republic's RUB 3,637. Because Kaliningrad is wealthier and smaller, this surge required only 2.6 percentage points more of

Kaliningrad's budget. In countries where lower levels of education are left to local governments, central governments often provide equalization grants to improve the equity of local spending on education for the young, but this is not the case for the Chuvash Republic and Kaliningrad.

IUE's data gathering and analysis serve a number of important purposes. They show other regions that budgets can be powerful instruments for reform in and of themselves, and in particular that shifting budgets to a focus on programs and objectives can accelerate reform. IUE's report is also useful for monitoring government priorities in two regions of a country that traditionally governs by setting rules rather than observing results. And IUE provides a window into civil society in the Russian Federation. The report provides a tremendously detailed analysis, but goes to great lengths to state its findings in such a neutral, even congratulatory, manner that the real message is often difficult to discern. The authors' keen awareness of their position allowed them to survive and produce a valuable report, given their unique environment. Nevertheless, the report documents impressive efforts by federal and regional governments to use some of the benefits of the Russian Federation's economic growth to begin rectifying its long neglect of the social sectors and provides real evidence of the importance of reforms below the federal level to improve government services.

Conclusion

To examine the effectiveness of government spending, an independent monitoring organization needs to gather information on government spending. But gathering information is not simply a means to an end: on its own, it can yield valuable insights into government transparency and performance. In some cases, it even reveals what the government knows, or does not know, about its own spending. And it reveals to what degree citizens can find out what their government is doing with their taxes.

This chapter also highlights another independent monitoring organization advantage. While independent monitoring organizations seem at a clear disadvantage in gathering budget information relative to external monitors, the organizations in this chapter turned their size and insider status into advantages, using their local knowledge to understand budgeting, even where they had uncertain legal rights to the information, even where the budgeting process seemed impenetrably complex, and even where the responsible officials seemed not to understand the process.

Gathering budget information is only the first step, however. Chapter 3 covers the next step, making sure that money goes where it is supposed to go after leaving government coffers.

Notes

1. Adamtey and others 2007.
2. Alvarado and Morón 2008.
3. Sumindar and others 2007.
4. BIGS analysts chose to examine Bandung, Banjar, and Sumedang because they have diverse experiences with budgeting for health and education. Banjar stands out for its exceptionally active mayor, a medical doctor, who meets regularly with citizens in "intensive meetings" and is particularly responsive to their demands. He deemed reinvigorating Banjar's tourism industry around Mustika Lake a priority and has lowered taxes to encourage investment in hotels and shopping centers. Bandung is West Java's administrative capital and is Indonesia's fourth largest and fastest growing city. It has the highest budget of any city in West Java, but its public services are widely criticized, and numerous reforms suggested to the city's mayor are repeatedly ignored. The city is ballooning in size, existing roads are insufficient to accommodate the increased traffic, and garbage management has become a problem. Sumedang is largely rural, with more than half its land used for agriculture. It has very active nongovernmental organizations, particularly in delivery of health services, and a high degree of citizen involvement, with organized forums held regularly to discuss problems.
5. BIGS is in good company in its conclusions on the existence and causes of wide variation in how well local governments provide services following decentralization (see, for example, Grindle 2007).
6. The yearly proportions were 29.5 percent in 2005, 30.3 percent in 2006, and 28.6 percent in 2007.
7. BIGS analysts note that Banjar's particularly active and responsive mayor is a medical doctor. Its administration was also the most efficient: it spent very little of its resources on the bureaucracy, freeing up more funds for use in service provision. Banjar's mayor has also prioritized propoor policies, including free healthcare and free education (it is the only one of the three cities that provides free education).
8. Rath, Madhusudhan, and Tarase 2007.
9. Toshniwal and Vyasulu 2008.
10. Institute for Urban Economics 2007.

Follow the money

Once independent monitoring organizations have gathered information on the budget, the next step is to trace the flow of money from the treasury to service delivery, verifying whether budgeted funds and resources are sent to their intended programs and projects on time and as needed. It is one thing for a government to allocate its resources well. It is quite another for the government to disburse those resources efficiently and effectively.

There are several potential problems with the flow of funds. Money bound for a health clinic is often handled by a chain of officials after leaving the treasury. It may need to wait repeatedly for a committee's approval or for an official to sign off. It may be subdivided and earmarked for specific tasks, such as salaries or infrastructure. Some money may be spent before reaching the clinic—on medicine or medical equipment, for example—by central procurement agencies. Some money may even be reallocated from its intended clinic to other priorities.

Nothing about this process is necessarily perverse. But each link in the chain is a chance for delay and waste and therefore requires attentive monitoring. Otherwise funds may be needlessly delayed while waiting for official signoff or whittled away as corrupt officials take their cuts. With each link civil servants' salaries drain resources from the delivery of services. Officials at higher levels may require side payments before releasing funds to lower levels. Authorities may allocate money ineffectively—for example, deciding to fund salaries without offering incentives to perform well. Centralized procurement agencies may fail to provide the supplies that service providers really need.

Uncovering delay and waste along the funding chain is rarely easy. The challenges are every bit as great as with gathering budget data. In investigating a funding delay, an independent monitoring organization may have to contend with a nearly impenetrable web of government bodies. Confusing procurement procedures may make it difficult to determine whether a supply shortage stems from funds that are misused or simply limited. Missing funds may be due to corruption or may simply be reporting errors.

The analytical skill required to make sense of such complexity, and thereby clarify problems with the flow of funds, may seem beyond the capacity of small independent monitoring organizations. But the four organizations profiled in this chapter did just that. Furthermore, they showed that independent monitoring organizations actually bring considerable advantages to this kind of analysis. Their analysts grew up with the government, so to them its various agencies are household names and its operations and effectiveness are common knowledge.

The four independent monitoring organizations in this chapter turned this familiarity to their advantage, using it to decipher complex funding streams. They investigated fund leakage and misuse, clarified seemingly incomprehensible webs of funding and procurement, and determined their consequences. And they did so by relying on the same local knowledge that, in chapter 2, helped them gather budget data. One found that funding for Peruvian health facilities is poorly allocated and held up at numerous points, undermining facilities' effective operation. Another found that Indonesian education funding, recently decentralized, is beset by numerous inefficiencies, from misinformation to delays and corruption. A third found that delays and poor recordkeeping in a Kenyan government scholarship program to help poor students afford secondary school suffers from so many inefficiencies that the program offers far less help and supports far fewer students than it should. A fourth found that, despite recent reforms to decentralize funding for Moldovan education, money is still allocated centrally using a formula that does not reflect local needs, and that schools rarely receive all the money that they are entitled to.

El Centro de Investigación de la Universidad del Pacífico, Peru

As shown in chapter 2, the challenge that the Research Center of the University of the Pacific (Centro de Investigación de la Universidad del Pacífico, CIUP) faced in following the money was complexity.[1] Money and resources flow from the Peruvian Health Ministry to health facilities through a convoluted web of agencies and streams. Simply understanding the web, let alone identifying its consequences, is a challenge. But CIUP analysts already knew a great deal about the system before beginning their analysis. This familiarity allowed them to quickly make sense of the flow of funds and to dig into the individual funding streams to identify several very serious problems. Their penetrating analysis is a powerful illustration of the gold mine that local knowledge offers analysts.

CIUP's goal was to investigate the budgetary bottlenecks to increasing access to healthcare. The previous chapter showed how even beginning to follow funding for two programs that are national priorities—tuberculosis prevention and control as well as immunization—revealed a complex, nontransparent web of funding that appears to leave health facilities with little discretion over their spending. As CIUP analysts followed the flow of funds for the immunization and tuberculosis programs through the budgeting process to service delivery, they discovered myriad roadblocks to effective spending as well as several layers of complexity that further reduce transparency and accountability. This section details those findings.

CIUP analysts investigated funding in 14 health centers in one of the five areas of Metropolitan Lima. Analysts surveyed the human resources staff for the area and more than 100 medical staff[2] at the 14 health centers about staff qualifications, availability of medical supplies, monitoring and supervision, insurance, and revenues.

The budget cycle

Peru's budget cycle has four major steps, which begin six months before the fiscal year starts and end six months after the fiscal year ends. Each is formulated in a way that appears to provide for transparency and accountability in appropriations and spending. But CIUP uncovered multiple structural factors that undermine effectiveness and accountability.

Step 1. Formulation and programming (end of May). Maximum expenditure proposals are approved for each ministry and program. CIUP found that the budget is heavily influenced by the previous year's budget and that changes are incremental at best, mainly because a large part of the budget (up to 70 percent) is devoted to fixed-cost items, such as salaries and pensions.

Step 2. Debate and appropriation (August–November). With maximum spending proposals set, the proposals are sent from the Ministry of Economy and Finance to Congress, where they are discussed and approved.

Step 3. Implementation (start of the new fiscal year). Based on the newly approved budget, allocations are made to all government units and subunits, which then implement the government's programs, projects, and policies. Much of the remainder of this section is devoted to CIUP's findings about bottlenecks and ineffectiveness at this stage.

Step 4. Evaluation (during and after project implementation). Actual expenses are reviewed in relation to those originally approved in the budget. However, evaluation is not judged by the output or product of the spending but simply by whether actual spending matched budgeted spending. Thus government units' incentive is simply to spend what they were given, even if the spending is ineffective or inefficient, to avoid cuts in their allocation in the next budget.

To evaluate this process in healthcare, CIUP concentrated on three major resource flows: money or cash, pharmaceuticals and medical supplies, and salaries. Chapter 2 described the intricate web through which resources flow from their sources down to health facilities (see figure 2.1 in chapter 2).

Money and cash

Monetary flows refer to resources allocated for nonpharmaceutical goods and services, primarily medical but also nonmedical costs related to improving health and sanitation (such as health education campaigns and preventative care). Monetary resources flow through the system in four ways:

- Funds are allocated to health directorates, networks, and hospitals by the Ministry of Economy and Finance, based on the Ministry of Health budget proposal.
- These entities combine the funds from the Ministry of Economy and Finance with funds from out-of-pocket fees paid by noninsured patients into a single budget for making purchases for their units and subunits.
- Petty cash is made available to health facilities for small expenses or emergency supplies.
- Each day, health facilities deposit the out-of-pocket fees they receive from noninsured patients into their health network's bank account.

CIUP found problems with each of these flows. The Ministry of Economy and Finance and civil society can keep track of general allocations of funds through the Integrated Financial Management System. Once funds are allocated to the expenditure units—the health directorates, networks, and hospitals—the units are authorized to hire personnel and purchase goods and services for themselves as well as for all health facilities under their control. But neither the directorates nor the networks make purchases until after receiving requests from health facilities, sometimes making the purchases a reimbursement to health facilities for expenses they have already incurred (such as maintenance expenses). This process repeats every month.

This purchasing process produces lengthy delays and leads to an obvious question: how does a facility pay for its needs before receiving reimbursement? CIUP found that health facility personnel rely on three informal mechanisms:

- For equipment and other goods and services, health facilities receive credit from suppliers. A function of the relationships between each facility and providers, this mechanism's success varies by health network.
- For services, personnel may put in extra hours, unpaid.
- For other necessary expenditures, personnel often dip into their own pockets. Some of these expenses can be reimbursed from petty cash, but the person in charge of petty cash can be absent from the facility for several days with no replacement.

This financing system gives health facilities little discretionary income—only petty cash, which comes with its own limits (small purchases of supplies or emergencies, not salaries or inventory). Health facilities cannot control any revenue from fees paid by noninsured patients; instead, they sort fees into two accounts—one for fees from the pharmacy and one for service fees, such as laboratory work or x-rays—and transfer the funds into the bank account of their health network. Facilities are allocated petty cash centrally by their health directorate and health network. CIUP found no clear rule or formula for these allocations. Analysts also found that they engender resentment among more active health facilities that produce higher incomes and feel they are subsidizing less active facilities.

Pharmaceuticals and related supplies

Most medicine and related supplies are purchased centrally—by the Ministry of Health and the health directorates—and sent to health facilities (see figure 2.1). This distribution system has numerous bottlenecks.

Problems begin with the first step in the process, when the Ministry of Health compiles what and how much the country's public health facilities and hospitals need. A unit within the ministry, DIGEMID, collects purchase requests and sends them to a separate procurement unit in the ministry for approval. The whole process is highly bureaucratic and can take weeks.

The process also leads to poor results. CIUP found poor coordination between the various units during the process, with health facilities rarely getting the pharmaceuticals they need. In the 14 health facilities examined in 2008, analysts found substantial delays and shortages of pharmaceuticals (table 3.1) and other essential medical supplies (table 3.2)—including those that reduce the risk of transmission

TABLE 3.1
Pharmaceutical shortages in 14 health facilities in Metropolitan Lima, Peru, 2008

Drug	Facilities with a shortage	Length of shortage (days)		
		Average	Maximum	Minimum
Amoxicillin 500 ml	5 (36%)	42	60	30
Amoxicillin	4 (29%)	60	90	30
Dicloxacillin 500 ml	3 (21%)	50	60	30
Parecetamol 500 ml tablet	2 (14%)	45	60	30
Ibuprofen 400 ml tablet	2 (14%)	45	45	45
Amoxicillin 250 ml	2 (14%)	38	45	30

Source: Alvarado and Morón 2008.

TABLE 3.2
Supply shortages in 14 health facilities in Metropolitan Lima, Peru, 2008

Supply item	Facilities with a shortage	Length of shortage (days)		
		Average	Maximum	Maximum
Bleach	7 (50%)	88	180	7
Gloves	4 (29%)	70	99	30
Cotton	3 (21%)	52	90	7
Office supplies	2 (14%)	75	90	60
Alcohol	2 (14%)	9	10	7
Gauze	2 (14%)	34	60	7
Tongue depressors	2 (14%)	30	30	30
Disinfectant	2 (14%)	49	90	7

Source: Alvarado and Morón 2008.

to facility personnel. Only 1 of the 14 facilities did not completely run out of supplies at least once in the previous year; some facilities were missing specific supplies for as long as six months. The severity of pharmaceutical shortages also varied widely: one facility reported no shortages, while another received just 25 percent of the pharmaceuticals it carries.

Supply shortages undermine treatment, particularly for tuberculosis—one of the two programs on which CIUP focused its analysis. For example, facilities that lack the full complement of diagnostic equipment—sputum glasses or other pharmaceutical goods—have a more difficult time preventing contagion, making effective treatment difficult and putting staff and other patients at risk. National data echo

CIUP's concern: analysts report that 18 of 33 health directorates across Peru did not have in inventory at least one of five pharmaceuticals used in the treatment of tuberculosis; 3 of the 18 lacked four. That means that more than half the health directorates were systematically undersupplied with medicines—for the treatment of a disease that is a designated national health priority. Such shortages do not engender optimism about the supply of medicines that are not given as high a priority.

Analysts investigated whether the shortages might reflect lack of communication between the health network and its facilities. In the tuberculosis program, for example, the health network provides facilities with needed supplies and tells the facilities when these supplies can be picked up. Tuberculosis medicines are provided under two plans: the primary plan and multidrug resistant plan. CIUP analysts asked both the health network and 12 of the study's health facilities several questions about the distribution of medicines under the two plans (table 3.3). Many times the responses differed. For example, the health network claimed to make all facilities aware of when to pick up medicines, but 5 of the 12 facilities claimed that they did not get that information under the primary plan and 7 claimed they did not get it under the multidrug resistant plan.

TABLE 3.3

Comparison of responses from the health network and 12 health facilities in Metropolitan Lima, Peru, about pharmaceuticals provided under the National Health Strategy for the Prevention and Control of Tuberculosis, 2008

Question	Health network responses		Facility responses	
	Primary plan	Multidrug resistant plan	Primary Plan	Multidrug resistant plan
Did the facilities have prior knowledge of pick-up dates?	Yes	Yes	Yes 7 (58%)	Yes 5 (42%)
			No **5 (42%)**	**No** **7 (58%)**
Was there a delay in the arrival of drugs during the last 12 months?	No	Yes	**Yes** **4 (33%)**	Yes 8 (67%)
			No 8 (67%)	**No** **4 (33%)**
Was there a shortage of tuberculosis medications during the last 12 months?	No	Yes	**Yes** **8 (67%)**	Yes 7 (58%)
			No 4 (33%)	**No** **5 (42%)**

Note: Bold numbers indicate where the responses of the health facility differed from those of the health network.

Source: Alvarado and Morón 2008.

Analysts repeated this analysis with the immunizations program, again uncovering substantial disagreements between the health network and the health facilities (table 3.4). For example, the health network reported a delay in the arrival of vaccines but not of needles, syringes, and other necessary inputs. The health facilities disagreed: 7 of the 14 reported no delay in the arrival of vaccines, while 4 reported a delay in the arrival of needles, syringes, and other inputs.

Salaries and human resources

The third resource flow that CIUP examined is the flow of resources to cover salaries, fringe benefits, and bonuses for medical and support staff in health facilities. Decisions about hiring and remuneration are made centrally by the health directorate and health network, so funds for salaries are allocated centrally; health facilities have no role. CIUP uncovered several problems with this process.

First, benefits and bonuses are determined by negotiations between unions and the national government, and health facility personnel are paid by their health directorate or health network through direct deposit into personal bank accounts. This leaves no room for locally judged merit pay. Even bonuses are determined centrally without regard to performance; those who receive a bonus are simply those who belong to the civil service—a little less than half of all medical personnel.

TABLE 3.4

Comparison of responses from the health network and 14 health facilities in Metropolitan Lima, Peru, about pharmaceuticals provided under the vaccination program, 2008

	Health network responses		Facility responses	
Question	Vaccines	Needles, syringes, and other inputs	Vaccines	Needles, syringes, and other inputs
Did the facilities have prior knowledge of the pick-up date?	Yes	Yes	Yes 11 (79%)	Yes 10 (71%)
			No 3 (21%)	**No 4 (29%)**
Was there a delay in the arrival of drugs during the last 12 months?	Yes	No	Yes 7 (50%)	**Yes 4 (29%)**
			No 7 (50%)	No 10 (71%)

Note: Bold numbers indicate where the responses of the health facility and the health network differed.

Source: Alvarado and Morón 2008.

Second, many facilities are understaffed, with requests to the Ministry of Health for additional personnel left unfilled. In the 14 health facilities that CIUP studied in 2008, the most pressing problem is a lack of doctors: 13 facilities reported requesting at least one additional doctor from the Ministry of Health, but only 7 received one. And doctors are only the beginning: the facilities reported being short of many other personnel, including nurses, midwives, and social workers (table 3.5).

In short, CIUP uncovered roadblocks to effective and efficient resource allocation at every stage of the funding process. Monetary resources are allocated centrally by a cumbersome and bureaucratic process that invites delays and often requires health facilities to depend on the generosity of suppliers and even dip into employees' own pockets to keep operating. The distribution of pharmaceuticals and medical supplies, purchased and distributed centrally, is also subject to numerous delays and miscommunications, leaving facilities short of key supplies, even for national priorities like tuberculosis treatment. Finally, salaries and bonuses are managed centrally, with no adjustment for merit, and numerous positions go unfilled despite requests to the Ministry of Health. The depth and frequency of problems suggest a need for vastly improved and simplified management and accountability arrangements in Peruvian healthcare.

TABLE 3.5

Success in filling personnel needs in 14 health facilities, in Metropolitan Lima, Peru, 2008

Personnel	Facilities that requested additional professionals		Facilities that received all they requested		Facilities that received some of what they requested		Facilities that did not receive any additional professionals	
	Number	Percent	Number	Percent	Number	Percent	Number	Percent
Doctors	13	100	7	54	1	8	5	38
Nurses	9	69	4	44	0	0	5	56
Midwives	4	31	3	75	0	0	1	25
Odontologists	3	23	1	33	0	0	2	67
Social workers	8	62	3	38	0	0	5	63
Psychologists	3	23	1	33	0	0	2	67
Other professionals or health technicians	8	62	3	38	1	13	4	50
Other administrative professionals or technicians	6	46	1	17	3	50	2	33

Source: Alvarado and Morón 2008.

Pusat Telaah dan Informasi Regional, Indonesia

The introduction to this chapter described several ways that funding can be wasted or delayed as it makes its way from the treasury to service providers. Indonesia's Centre for Regional Information and Studies (Pusat Telaah dan Informasi Regional, PATTIRO) set out to examine them all in one of the most ambitious studies in this book.[3] The sheer breadth of PATTIRO's project is powerful evidence that independent monitoring organizations are fully capable of examining the flow of funds both rigorously and usefully.

As mentioned in the discussion of the Bandung Institute of Governance Studies in the previous chapter, Indonesia has become one of the world's most decentralized countries. Largely because of transfers from the central government, Indonesia's provinces and districts spend 36 percent of public funds, a higher proportion than the average for both Organisation for Economic Co-operation and Development countries and all East Asian countries except China.[4] PATTIRO wanted to evaluate the many schemes that fund local schools, including central government transfer schemes and locally generated funds, and found numerous problems with the distribution of money for operating expenses and investment. The method used to allocate funding is often confusing and opaque. Funding arrives late, is sometimes less than promised, and leaks out at several points along the way as gifts and bribes. Money is also frequently not spent on what it was intended for, reporting on spending is inaccurate, and auditing is cursory at best. PATTIRO's findings leave no doubt about serious weaknesses in the decentralization of education funding in Indonesia.

PATTIRO analysts focused on seven financing schemes in 38 elementary and secondary primary schools in two Indonesian regions: Serang Regency, in Central Java, and Gresik Regency, in East Java. Before PATTIRO's findings are discussed, some background on seven financing schemes that fund local education in Indonesia is needed. The seven schemes fall into two general categories: three fund operating expenses and four fund capital investment. Of the three that fund operating expenses, two are operated by provincial governments: the school operational assistance scheme (BOS) and the operational assistance for textbook purchases scheme (Textbook BOS). The third is a district-funded school operational assistance scheme (Local BOS). The four capital investment schemes are block grants, which are provided by the central government to fund investments in both elementary and secondary schools; a specific allocation fund (*dana alokasi khusus*, DAK), which is funds provided by the central government to district governments for renovating elementary schools; deconcentrated funds (Dekon), which are provided by provincial governments to fund renovations of elementary and secondary schools;

and the local renovation budget, which is district-level funding for renovating both elementary and secondary schools.

Not all of the 38 schools PATTIRO surveyed in 2008 received funds from all seven schemes; in fact, the only two schemes that covered all 38 were the operational expenses schemes BOS and Textbook BOS. Of the 38 schools, 20 received funding under Local BOS, 13 under DAK, 13 from the local renovation budgets, 8 from block grants, and 7 from Dekon. PATTIRO wanted to understand the problems that schools might face in receiving financing through these seven schemes, and it concentrated on seven potential problems (table 3.6).

TABLE 3.6

Problems with the seven school funding schemes covering 38 elementary and secondary primary schools in Serang Regency and Gresik Regency, Indonesia, 2007

Problem or phase	Capital investment schemes				Operational schemes			Percent of projects
	DAK	Dekon	Block grants	Local renovation	BOS	Local BOS	Textbook BOS	
Total projects	13	7	8	13	38	20	38	100
Expenditure plan does not match priority school needs	4	4	2	6	0	0	0	12
Delay in transfer of fund	0	0	0	0	38	20	0	42
Abuse of transfer regulation	4	2	0	0	0	0	0	4
Unplanned funding cut	0	0	0	0	20	20	0	29
Actual expenditures do not match the planned/regulated expenditures	3	2	0	7	—	—	—	29
Reduced results/ quality compared with the price	7	4	0	10	—	—	—	51
Funding leakage								
Allocation phase	8	4	4	9	0	0	0	18
Transfer phase	4	2	0	0	8	12	0	26
Spending phase	5	6	4	8	38	20	11	68
Reporting or audit phase	4	4	0	6	22	12	6	39

— indicates that the fund was not tracked.

Source: Septyandrica 2008.

First, analysts wanted to know whether schools were receiving money according to their needs. Each year schools are asked to draw up a list of priorities. Some schools' greatest need is to renovate classrooms; others need to build new classrooms or playing fields. But schools often do not receive funds for what they need—for example, one school in the Serang District asked for money to renovate classrooms and instead received funds to build a 100 meter fence (even though the school's perimeter was 500 meters). Such mismatches were common in all four capital investment schemes and were most common in the local and provincial schemes. Four of the seven schools that received Dekon funding had this problem, as did six of the thirteen that received money from the local renovation budget, four of the thirteen schools that received DAK funds, and two of the eight schools that received block grants. None of the schemes that funded operating expenses had this problem (see table 3.6).

Second, analysts asked whether funds arrived late. They found that funds arrived on time with every transfer from the four capital investment schemes (DAK, Dekon, block grants, and the local renovation budget) and from Textbook BOS, but arrived late in every transfer from BOS and Local BOS. For example, Local BOS funds in the Gresik region always arrived late, usually by three months; BOS funding in the Serang region faced a similar delay. The analysts discovered that the delays are caused by the bank transfer mechanisms used to distribute BOS money. During delays two-thirds of schools resorted to borrowing money from school cooperatives; others had to turn to outside sources. These loans require interest payments, which create an additional problem, since operational financing schemes do not consider interest payments a legitimate expense.

Third, analysts studied whether the method of transfer conformed to the transfer regulation. Money is supposed to be transferred into school bank accounts, but in four of the thirteen DAK transfers and two of the seven DAK transfers respondents reported that they received the money in cash. This was not a problem with the other schemes.

Fourth, analysts investigated whether schools received all the money they were promised. As with funds arriving late, only the two operating expense schemes, BOS and Local BOS, had this problem. But for those two it was serious: schools would plan at the start of the year to receive a certain amount, and that amount would end up being cut. Twenty of the thirty-eight schools receiving funding through the BOS scheme and all twenty schools receiving funding through the Local BOS scheme experienced unplanned cuts in funding. The reasons for these unplanned cuts differed. In one case a six-month fund was cut so that schools received only five months of funding. Because of a technical error, all the schools in the Gresik region receiving BOS funding had their funding cut in December 2007—by up to 5,000 rupees per student (about $0.54, or 15–23 percent of per student transfers, depending on whether the school was an elementary or secondary school). Analysts learned that fixing the error would have taken a lot of time and required legislative approval, so local governments simply cut the per student allocation.

Fifth, analysts checked whether the capital investment money spent by a school matched what was planned or required. Funds matched only with the block grant scheme. In 7 of the 13 local renovation budget cases, 2 of the 7 Dekon cases, and 3 of the 13 DAK cases, school spending diverged from the financing schemes' regulations or from the original plans. To explain these divergences, schools argued that they were trying to meet more pressing needs. For example, money meant to renovate classrooms was instead used to build lavatories, libraries, or offices for teachers.

Sixth, analysts examined whether schools were getting their money's worth from their capital investment spending. This seemed to be the case with block grant funding, but with most transfers under DAK and Dekon and from the local renovation budget, schools reported paying more than they planned for capital investment or feeling that the quality of what they received did not match the cost. Most respondents claimed that their buildings were worth only 50–70 percent of their budgeted value.

Seventh, analysts wanted to know about leakage of funding—that is, discrepancies in the funding reported at each phase of the transfer process that could be due to simple accounting errors or to corruption. Schools were asked about leakages in four phases of the transfer process: allocation, transfer, spending, and reporting or auditing.

Leakages were a problem with every scheme, but the phase during which funding leaked varied. At the allocation phase, funding leaked in at least half of transfers under all four capital investment schemes, most often for payoffs to influential persons in policymaking to secure capital investment financing; this money was used for lobbying, proposal processing, and hiring consultants. Respondents claimed that such expenses accounted for up to 10 percent of the budget. At the transfer phase money was sometimes spent as "gratitude money" for people involved in the transfer, such as bank and post office employees. These leakages were most common in Local BOS transfers—they were reported in 12 of the 20 transfers—and in some DAK, Dekon, and BOS transfers. At the spending phase leakages were reported in every scheme. Some 68 percent of transfers saw leakage, including every one of the transfers under BOS and Local BOS.

PATTIRO found that it was common for the schools to give money to those conducting the audit or otherwise monitoring the spending. Funding leaked during reporting or auditing in 40 percent of transfers; only block grants did not see this type of leakage.

In short, PATTIRO's comprehensive analysis presents a damning picture of the flow of operational and investment expenditures from government coffers to schools. Allocations are confusing, and funding is sometimes less than promised, often arrives late, and leaks out along the way to pay for gifts and bribes.[5]

Institute of Policy Analysis and Research, Kenya

In 1994 the Kenyan government started a secondary education bursary scheme to help economically vulnerable groups cope with the rising cost of secondary education. The Institute of Policy Analysis and Research (IPAR), a public policy research organization in Nairobi, wanted to know whether the scheme was being funded efficiently and effectively.[6] The answer, based on their thorough analysis, is an unequivocal no. IPAR found that funding often arrives late and that substantial discrepancies exist between amounts allocated and amounts received—discrepancies that may illustrate poor recordkeeping or corruption. As a result of this inefficiency, the system provides less help to fewer students than it could.

As a result of decentralization in 2003, local Constituency Bursary Fund Committees[7] administer the scholarship scheme and select recipients under the guidance of the national Ministry of Education. Under this arrangement the ministry specifies evaluation criteria and scholarship amounts, and the committees evaluate the applications and award the scholarships. IPAR surveyed the principals of all 49 public secondary schools in Nairobi as well as the committees in Nairobi's eight constituencies (districts)—Dagoretti, Embakasi, Kamukunji, Kasarani, Lang'ata, Makadara, Starehe, and Westlands—and held focus groups with student beneficiaries in 32 of the 49 schools.

Delayed disbursements

Bursary funds are supposed to be available for students prior to the start of each secondary school term in August, December, and April, meaning that funds should be disbursed in July, November, and March. But the reality is far different. Funds are disbursed in phases whose number and timing vary widely across constituencies (table 3.7). Money is often not even allocated until just before or even after the start of term, and there is usually a substantial lag—up to 99 days—before the money is actually disbursed. Only Kamukunji had a lag of less than 10 days. IPAR analysts discovered a simple cause of this delay: more than a third (37.5 percent) of committees met to consider applications after the funds had been received—and evaluating applications takes at least two weeks.

TABLE 3.7

Disbursement amounts and dates for Nairobi's eight constituencies, 2007

Constituency	Phase	Amount allocated (Kenyan shillings)	Date allocated	Amount disbursed (Kenyan shillings)	Date disbursed
Dagoretti	Phase 1	1,846,437	January 25, 2007	1,821,437	March 23, 2007
	Phase 2	1,846,437	May 7, 2007	1,821,437	July 27, 2007
Embakasi	Phase 1	3,153,069	February 5, 2007	3,735,000	February 27, 2007
	Phase 2	3,153,069	May 14, 2007	3,330,000	May 28, 2007
Kamukunji	Phase 1	1,174,716	February 28, 2007	1,180,000	March 5, 2007
	Phase 2	1,174,716	May 30, 2007	1,160,000	June 8, 2007
Kasarani	Phase 1	2,755,276	January 25, 2007	2,560,000	February 26, 2007
	Phase 2	2,755,276	May 28, 2007	2,790,000	June 26, 2007
Lang'ata	Phase 1	697,000	March 31, 2007	697,000	April 15, 2007
	Phase 2	1,200,000	April 30, 2007	1,200,000	May 15, 2007
	Phase 3	1,110,000	July 31, 2007	1,110,000	August 26, 2007
	Phase 4	300,000	November 30, 2007	300,000	December 20, 2007
Makadara	Phase 1	2,571,055	February 8, 2007	2,625,250	May 6, 2007
	Phase 2[a]	2,571,055	May 15, 2007	2,292,450	August 22, 2007
				300,000	November 22, 2007
Starehe	Phase 1	1,533,000	—	1,533,000	—
	Phase 2	1,500,000	—	1,500,000	—
Westlands	Phase 1	973,540	February 2007	1,020,000	March 2007
	Phase 2	973,540	May 2007	935,000	July 2007

— is not allocated or disbursed.

a. Although the constituency received the phase 2 funds on the same date, it disbursed them in two tranches.

Source: Kibua and others 2008.

These delays are a serious problem for beneficiaries because students who cannot pay school fees are sent home to raise the necessary funds. Even when funds are disbursed only a few days late, students must still miss their first few days of class. In focus groups every beneficiary reported being forced to make numerous trips to officials for information on when funds would be disbursed.

Leakage and recording errors

IPAR analysts also found discrepancies between amounts allocated and amounts disbursed. Some constituencies disburse too little, some too much. Discrepancies like these appear throughout IPAR's findings. The number of students that Ministry of Education data show receiving benefits differed greatly from the number actually receiving benefits (as determined by IPAR's surveys; table 3.8). In Lang'ata, for example, IPAR determined the number of beneficiaries in 2004 to be 238, while Ministry of Education data show 397. In most cases ministry data show more beneficiaries than IPAR found. In 2006, for example, the ministry reported 52 percent more beneficiaries than IPAR found. Yet in a few cases ministry data show fewer beneficiaries than IPAR found: in 2004 in the Kasarani constituency, for example, IPAR found 919 beneficiaries, while ministry data showed only 215. Because discrepancies run in both directions, it is hard to tell whether they are simply recording errors or signs of corruption.

TABLE 3.8

Number of scholarship beneficiaries, according to IPAR and the Kenyan Ministry of Education, 2004–07

	2004		2005		2006		2007	
Constituency	IPAR	Ministry	IPAR	Ministry	IPAR	Ministry	IPAR	Ministry
Dagoretti	769	167	676	—	748	1,168	930	830
Embakasi	—	1,608	368	—	860	838	1,202	1,188
Kamukunji	—	664	202	—	305	664	401	401
Kasarani	919	215	963	—	771	766	909	908
Lang'ata	238	397	328	—	351	879	599	687
Makadara	—	—	1,010	—	1,225	1,773	804	758
Starehe	—	812	411	—	428	879	478	472
Westlands	—	584	—	—	215	469	345	295
Total	1,926	4,447	3,958	—	4,903	7,436	5,668	5,539

— is not available.

Source: Kibua and others 2008.

Unsurprisingly, there are similar discrepancies in the disbursements that IPAR measured and those in ministry records (table 3.9). Again the differences are often enormous. For instance, in 2004 IPAR found disbursements in Lang'ata constituency to be KES 1.3 million, while ministry records show KES 3.3 million.

Because IPAR's numbers show that more money is sometimes disbursed than ministry records show, it is possible that discrepancies are simply recording errors. But IPAR's interviews and focus groups suggest that at least some discrepancies are the result of leakage. In a fifth of the schools where IPAR conducted interviews, respondents reported funds being allocated to students who were no longer in school. In another 27 percent of schools students received scholarships from more than one constituency. When faced with these situations, 6 percent of respondents reported returning the funds to the committee's account, 4 percent reported holding the money in the school's account, and 18 percent reported reallocating the funds to other students in need.

The delays and poor recordkeeping that IPAR uncovered seriously affect the scholarship scheme. Delays mean that students do not get their needed funds on time and therefore start their courses late and waste valuable time visiting education offices in the hope of speeding the process. The substantial differences between ministry records and IPAR's findings suggest at the very least shoddy recordkeeping and possibly something more sinister.[8] IPAR's findings point to the need for serious reform;[9] if the scheme distributed its money with fewer errors, it could easily serve more students more adequately.

TABLE 3.9

Scholarship disbursements, according to IPAR and the Kenyan Ministry of Education, 2004–07 (Kenyan shillings)

	2004		2005		2006		2007	
Constituency	IPAR	Ministry	IPAR	Ministry	IPAR	Ministry	IPAR	Ministry
Dagoretti	1,130,000	981,000	4,519,057	—	3,298,378	3,111,000	3,642,874	3,304,000
Embakasi	5,587,776	5,587,776	2,465,000	—	6,555,000	5,908,000	7,065,000	6,765,000
Kamukunji	1,675,799	1,675,799	3,373,400	—	2,340,000	3,383,000	1,753,000	2,340,000
Kasarani	4,259,230	989,000	5,209,265	—	5,406,000	4,017,000	5,510,552	5,260,000
Lang'ata	1,346,400	3,318,155	1,704,000	—	1,763,000	3,575,750	3,307,000	3,902,000
Makadara	3,641,799	3,641,799	3,876,160	—	4,479,920	4,418,914	5,217,700	5,068,500
Starehe	2,803,000	2,618,407	1,368,000	—	2,955,000	3,805,500	3,033,000	3,019,000
Westlands	2,358,773	2,358,773	2,920,000	—	2,821,000	2,821,000	1,955,000	2,130,000
Total	22,802,777	21,170,709	25,434,882	—	29,618,298	31,040,164	31,484,126	31,788,500

— is not available.

Source: Kibua and others 2008.

Institute for Development and Social Initiatives, Moldova

Many of the independent monitoring organizations supported by the Transparency and Accountability Project focused on the success of recent reforms to social programs, such as decentralization or results-based budgeting. The Institute for Development and Social Initiatives (IDIS) Viitorul in Moldova is one such organization. IDIS set out to assess the extent and effect of decentralization in Moldova's education system as well as the general state of financing for education.[10] Analysts examined budget data and laws as well as national and international reports, and interviewed mayors, local government officials, and the directors and vice-directors of 30 schools chosen to represent a broad swath of Moldova's education system.[11] They found that Moldovan education budgeting remains centralized and is allocated by a system that is vulnerable to politics and that creates vast inequities in funding.

IDIS found that power over the Moldovan education budget rests mostly with the Ministry of Finance; local governments, and even the Ministry of Education, have little say. While education is nominally the responsibility of local governments (*raioane*), the Ministry of Finance pays teachers directly and draws up annual funding norms, based on enrollments, that cover local expenditure over most aspects of education.[12] The Ministry of Education provides data on the number of students, which the Ministry of Finance uses to calculate the required spending for maintenance, utilities, teacher salaries (which are specifically earmarked and account for 70–90 percent of a school's budget[13]), and management. Funds are transferred to regional governments, which distribute them to *raioane*.[14] Mayors and school directors thus have little control over their schools' budgets.

The centralized per student funding structure creates myriad inequalities. Small schools are particularly hard hit, since schools incur certain fixed costs regardless of how many students they enroll. But these inequalities are only the beginning. The funds that eventually reach schools rarely cover all their expenses, particularly after paying teachers. The Ministry of Finance calculates schools' budgets by their enrollment, but schools pay teachers by the hour. And in practice the Ministry of Finance does not transfer all of what the funding norms call for. In 2008, 60 percent of Moldovan schools received less than they should have under Ministry of Finance norms, and 29 of the 30 schools that IDIS surveyed reported that the money they received did not cover their costs. Interviews with the 30 school directors suggest that heating and school maintenance use up almost half their nonsalary budgets. School directors also report rarely receiving budgetary allocations for school refurbishing or repairs. In fact, capital expenditures account for only 5 percent of the national education budget and are allocated to repair only about 40–50 schools annually.

To compensate, schools often turn to foreign aid, as well as their communities—which naturally disadvantages schools in poorer areas. The 30 school directors report that the average annual parental contribution is 1,000–2,000 lei ($90–$180), or 2.5–5.0 percent of household income in Moldova. In some schools parent–teacher associations provide all the textbooks, and in 25 of the 30 schools the parent–teacher association funds repairs and improvements, such as new equipment and furniture. Some parent–teacher associations pay for utilities, but some schools do not have parent–teacher associations.

Regional governments also try to compensate for shortfalls and inequities in funding, typically by deviating from the Ministry of Finance's norms to transfer money from schools that receive closer to their actual costs to schools with shortfalls. But this involves negotiation between local and regional governments, heavily influenced by personal relationships and politics. IDS found that a school director with a poor relationship with the local government has difficulty getting additional funding. Half the 30 school directors IDIS interviewed reported strained relationships with their local governments. Indeed, actual funding per student varies wildly. In 2008 the Ministry of Finance's per student funding norm was 3,483 lei (about $313), but IDIS reports that actual funding ranged from 2,631 lei to 11,241 lei.

In all, IDIS concludes that education funding in Moldova is highly centralized, allocated by a formula that creates inequality and fails to provide many schools with what they need, and heavily influenced by politics.

Conclusion

Just because a government has budgeted sufficient funds for health or education does not mean that those funds are disbursed efficiently and effectively. This chapter has highlighted the efforts of four independent monitoring organizations to determine whether the money and other resources that their country's government budgeted for a service actually made it to service delivery—in full, as needed, and on time. Analyzing these funding flows is rarely easy: independent monitoring organizations face a web of agencies, funding streams, and conflicting government reports, many of which seem specifically designed to thwart clarification. Making sense of it all may appear beyond the capacity of small local independent monitoring organizations, but the four organizations highlighted in this chapter proved extremely capable of following money as it flowed from the treasury to frontline service providers and—more important—of identifying the problems with these flows.

One secret behind this success is their existing knowledge of the system. The analysts did not need to learn the funding streams from scratch. In fact, these four independent monitoring organizations, like all 16 in this book, completed their analyses in just five months—a speed that, given the complexities they encountered, would not have been possible without a basic understanding of what to look for.

The success of the organizations also reflects the kind of commitment that comes from having something at stake. Only the most dedicated analysts would wade into the funding thickets described in this chapter. The analysts in this chapter did it because these thickets affect the success of their schools and their health clinics. The day IPAR analysts finished their study of the Kenyan secondary scholarship scheme, they did not fly to Washington or London to present their findings. They went home to their families, to their children who may one day apply for a government scholarship to attend secondary school. Later, they shared their findings with neighbors who have children in the same position and with local newspapers. And next year, when the scholarship funds are again disbursed, they and the other citizens that they informed can watch not just with new knowledge about the bottlenecks that delay and disrupt those funds but also with a vested interest in seeing that those bottlenecks are reduced.

Notes

1. Alvarado and Morón 2008.
2. Staff included the head doctor; pharmacists; individuals responsible for the National Strategies for Tuberculosis and Vaccinations; the lab specialist; the store room administrator; human resources coordinators (nurses or administrative assistants); the petty cash, goods, and services (logística) coordinator (in most cases administrative technicians); the general cashier; the pharmacy cashier; and national health insurance administrative assistants. Surveys varied by the interviewee's position.
3. Septyandrica 2008.
4. Most of the money spent by local governments is transferred from the central government. Local revenue accounts for only 15–20 percent of their spending.
5. Although outside the scope of this chapter, PATTIRO found equally serious problems with spending: money is frequently not spent on what it was intended for, reporting is inaccurate, and auditing is cursory at best. For example, 70 percent of PATTIRO's respondents claimed that they used some BOS money for things other than planned expenditures. One school reported using funds to purchase a lawn mower and to build a bridge near the school—although neither expense was covered by BOS funding. Some 65 percent of respondents claimed they diverted money because of urgent needs, another 15 percent said that they were simply uninformed of the regulations, and the remaining respondents blamed the misuse of funds on school management.
6. Kibua and others 2008.

7. Each committee has a maximum of 16 members, a third of them women, and includes the area's member of parliament, the area's education officer, three representatives of religious organizations, two chairpersons of parent–teacher associations of two secondary schools, the chairperson of the board of governors, a councillor, a district officer, a representative of an educational nongovernmental organization or community-based organization, a local representative from the Kenya National Union of Teachers, and two head teachers, one of whom must be from a girls' secondary school.

8. IPAR cites substantial anecdotal evidence that many beneficiaries who should not qualify for the bursary receive money anyway because of political reasons.

9. In other aspects of the study not considered here, IPAR found that the number of beneficiaries from the bursary scheme is far lower than needed and that most beneficiaries receive far less money than needed to cover their fees. In six constituencies 2,937 beneficiaries (84.2 percent) received awards worth KES 5,000, 539 (15.4 percent) received awards worth KES 10,000, and 14 (0.4 percent) received the maximum KES 15,000 award. Secondary school fees, which are regulated by the Kenyan government, are set at a maximum of KES 10,500 for day schools, KES 22,900 for boarding schools, and KES 28,900 for national schools.

10. Munteanu and others 2008.

11. IDIS chose schools that varied by regional location (south, center, north), type of community (small, average, large), ethnicity (Moldovan, Ukrainian, Russian, and Gagauzian languages taught in schools), and level (primary, secondary). In each school analysts conducted two or three interviews with directors and vice-directors. Interviews centered on a questionnaire IDIS developed to gather data on budgetary issues, wages, repairs, students, and maintenance costs. Data collected were cross-checked with mayors and executive authorities of communes, villages, or cities.

12. IDIS found that local governments are not just impotent in funding. The national and regional (intermediate-level) governments are together responsible for setting up new schools, supervising *raioane* education departments, staffing school directors, making capital investments and repairs, training teachers, and selecting curriculum. Local governments are responsible only for conducting maintenance and paying salaries (with funds earmarked by the Ministry of Finance). In addition, IDIS found legal confusion about the responsibilities of various levels of governments, with some levels seeming to have overlapping responsibilities.

13. Yet salaries are dismal: in 2008 they were only 60 percent of average Moldovan wages, the lowest relative to the average wage since the fall of the Soviet Union in 1991.

14. Per student funding was introduced in 1998; before then schools were given funds earmarked for specific activities (salaries, maintenance, and so on), and funds earmarked

for one purpose could not be used for another. In 2005 the Ministry of Finance began paying teachers directly.

Chapter 4

Examine the spending

Once resources make it out of the treasury and through the bureaucracy, they end up in the hands of service providers, where they finally have the chance to improve lives. Determining whether they actually do is the next step for independent monitoring organizations. Are there enough resources to do the job? Are they being used efficiently and effectively? Are services widely available? When most people think of improving government services, these are the sorts of questions they usually ask. The point where resources become services is also the point that provides the most tangible sense of how well a government is using its resources.

Analysis of service delivery is also where the skills, interests, and "ear to the ground" orientation of independent monitoring organizations are most valuable. The first three organizations highlighted in this chapter studied absenteeism. Independent monitoring organization analysts live in the areas that they study, so they are able to show up unannounced at a school or clinic to record absenteeism and can check their findings with a follow-up visit the next day—or three months later. All the organizations highlighted in this chapter developed standard forms and methods to record absenteeism, but they also supplemented these with nonstandardized interviews and focus groups in local vernaculars. Depending on the politics, they could operate either under the government's radar or in close and mutually beneficial collaboration with the government. And using these techniques, all three discovered astonishing rates of absenteeism. In three Ghanaian school districts almost half the teachers were absent at least once during the week analysts visited; in two districts in Buenos Aires students lose an average of 49 days out of the 180 day school year because of teacher absenteeism and school closures; and in one Kenyan district absenteeism among healthcare workers reached 25 percent, costing the government more than $1 million a year.

This chapter also describes the work of two independent monitoring organizations that examined the efficacy of government spending in other ways: by measuring the adequacy, equity, and financing of services and the satisfaction of beneficiaries. Their studies also highlight important advantages to independent monitoring organizations' work. Analysts from these organizations began their work already knowing, in detail born of long experience, how the programs they were investigating operated and what needs they were supposed to fill. One study demonstrates that an independent monitoring organization need not produce only negative findings. The organization found that several Guatemalan programs intended to keep children in school are poorly and inefficiently funded but are otherwise equitable and satisfy most beneficiaries. The other discovered that many Polish hospitals are able to provide quality care without going into debt and analyzed four cases that suggest ways for indebted hospitals to control their costs.

Together the five organizations in this chapter exemplify the book's central theme: independent monitoring organizations bring many advantages to the monitoring and analysis of service delivery. Although gathering the data and following the money are vital steps, examining spending provides the clearest picture of the effectiveness of government service delivery—and, not coincidentally—some of the clearest examples of these advantages.

Center for Democratic Development, Ghana

This chapter begins with three studies about absenteeism—two of teachers, one of healthcare workers. The first is from Ghana's Center for Democratic Development (CDD). Like all low-income countries, Ghana has very limited resources to devote to education, and the global recession means that resources have become even scarcer. In 2004 Ghana spent approximately $300 per student, more than 98 percent of which funded teacher salaries, leaving only $5.40 to cover the remaining costs of educating each student.[1] Teacher absenteeism therefore wastes most of the money Ghana spends on education, and with few other educational resources, there is no substitute for a missing teacher. Moreover, because knowledge accumulates over time, students' knowledge and future potential are degraded exponentially when they do not have regular access to a teacher.[2]

CDD's goal was simple: to understand the extent of and reasons for teacher absenteeism.[3] The results are appalling: in one week CDD analysts found that 47 percent of teachers in the surveyed schools were absent at least once. But CDD analysts did not stop there, digging deeper into the reasons for absenteeism. Many turned out to be surprisingly benign and might easily be fixed. Many teachers, for example, missed class because they had to travel long distances to pick up their paychecks or to attend official training workshops held by the Ghana Education Service.

CDD collected data on teacher absenteeism in 30 public primary schools in three districts using specially designed surveys[4] and stratified random sampling to ensure representation of a variety of school characteristics in the survey districts.[5] The team surveyed teachers and head teachers to collect data on teacher and school characteristics.[6] They then made unannounced return visits to the schools and recorded teacher attendance on tally sheets. Analysts classified a teacher as absent if they could not physically locate the teacher in the school during official school hours. These visits covered both morning and afternoon periods, with most schools receiving at least two visits.

Patterns of absenteeism

CDD identified some clear patterns in the absenteeism data. One was the days of the week when teachers were absent. Absenteeism followed a U-shaped pattern: 24 percent of the 192 teachers surveyed were absent on Monday, but only 12 percent on Tuesday; by Thursday, however, absenteeism had risen again to 31 percent and reached a high of 40 percent on Friday (figure 4.1). More male teachers than female teachers were absent at least once (50 percent compared with 41 percent; table 4.1). Absenteeism was also slightly higher in urban schools than in rural schools, as was the frequency of absence (20 percent of teachers in urban schools were absent at least twice, compared with 15 percent in rural schools). And 2 percent of all teachers and 3 percent of urban teachers were absent for the entire week.[7]

Absence rates were also higher among professional teachers: 57 percent were absent at least once during CDD's fieldwork, and 22 percent were absent at least twice, whereas only 36 percent of nonprofessional teachers were absent at least once and only 9 percent were absent at least twice. CDD analysts posited that job security may be the underlying reason: the jobs of professional teachers are more secure than those of nonprofessionals, and pay is based largely on length of service, so there is little incentive in the compensation system to perform well.

Additional correlates of absenteeism

CDD investigated several additional factors that might correlate with absenteeism: school infrastructure and facilities, proximity of schools to services such as clinics and bus stops, and supervision.[8] For example, only 21 percent of teachers in schools with common staff rooms were absent once or more during the week of fieldwork, compared with 53 percent in schools without them. Parental supervision also seems

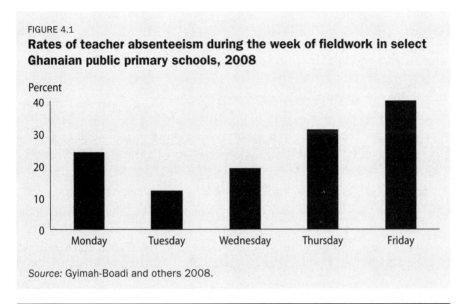

FIGURE 4.1

Rates of teacher absenteeism during the week of fieldwork in select Ghanaian public primary schools, 2008

Source: Gyimah-Boadi and others 2008.

TABLE 4.1

Frequency of absenteeism during the week of fieldwork in select Ghanaian public primary schools, by gender and urban or rural location, 2008 (percent)

Rate of absenteeism	Overall	Male	Female	Rural	Urban
Never absent	53	50	59	54	50
Absent once	30	35	23	31	30
Absent twice	10	9	11	8	17
Absent three times	3	2	7	4	0
Absent four times	2	2	0	2	0
Absent five times	2	2	0	1	3

Source: Gyimah-Boadi and others 2008.

to be associated with lower absenteeism: 57 percent of teachers in schools without an active parent–teacher association were absent at least once during the week of fieldwork, compared with 45 percent of teachers in schools with a parent–teacher association. Analysts found support for this finding in focus group discussions with parent–teacher associations during which parents were enthusiastic about the development of quality schools in their communities. Surprisingly, proximity to an official supervisor's office seemed to be uncorrelated with teacher absenteeism. In fact, CDD found that the Ghana Education Service, which employs and supervises teachers, is ineffective at supervision and perhaps even complicit in absenteeism: only 57 percent of interviewed teachers reported that circuit supervisors visit their schools once a month; in rural areas 13 percent receive visits from supervisors only once in a three-month term; and 3 percent of teachers in rural schools reported never having seen their circuit supervisor.

Speculating on the causes of absenteeism

In addition to quantitative analysis, CDD analysts interviewed head teachers[9] and reviewed teacher logbooks, which teachers are supposed to sign as they enter and leave the school. In fact, the logbooks provided little information: teachers often signed in but did not sign out, so it was unclear when they left. In the few cases where teachers indicated reasons for leaving early or arriving late, the most common were medical checkups, going to the bank, and official duties at the district education office. Others indicated "gone to town/city" without any details.

When asked, 75 percent of head teachers downplayed teacher absenteeism in their schools. For example, one head teacher, who was described by the local parent–teacher association as frequently absent and who was indeed absent three times during the week of fieldwork, vehemently denied that teacher absenteeism was a problem.

But the interviews with head teachers still provided additional insight into absenteeism, including some factors not captured by the quantitative analysis. When pressed, head teachers—or other teachers who responded when the head teacher was absent—reported that major causes of teacher absence are sickness and medical checkups (82 percent of 28 respondents); salary collection (57 percent); attending funerals (46 percent); maternity leave, attending to emergency family issues, and official business at the district education office (11 percent each); attending distance learning lectures and lack of transport (7 percent each); and bad roads, Friday prayers by Muslims, lack of accommodations, and poor teaching and learning materials (4 percent each). The interviews also found that teachers frequently assume other sizable responsibilities within the community, such as religious leadership, community liaison with international nongovernmental organizations, or local government representatives. These responsibilities may take them away from the classroom, sometimes for long periods.

Some of these factors may not be difficult to address. Salary collection accounts for such a large portion of absence because teachers must go in person to receive their salary from a bank, and banks are generally located in district or regional capitals, as much as half a day's journey from rural schools. The high absence rate recorded in the latter part of the week, and especially on Fridays, is largely attributable to two causes: funerals and a distance learning program's lectures scheduled on Fridays. Funerals are usually large community events, and schools often decide independently to close entirely when a funeral is held in the community. During the week of fieldwork, three schools were closed for funerals. Distance education lectures are potentially easier to remedy. According to the Ministry of Finance, about 18,000 teachers are participating in a government-sponsored higher education program that holds lectures on weekends (Ghana Ministry of Finance 2008). Although the lectures begin on Friday after school hours are over, many teachers live far from where the classes are held and must therefore skip school on Friday to arrive on time. With so many teachers participating, CDD speculates that the program is likely to significantly contribute to absenteeism nationwide.

In fact, in chapter 6, which discusses advocacy and dissemination, CDD's findings about absenteeism, and some of its simple and easily preventable causes, are shown to have truly struck a chord in Ghana. Six major newspapers published stories on CDD's report, and the director of basic education at the Ghana Education Service is already taking steps to reorganize the distance learning program to make it less disruptive.

Centro de Implementación de Políticas Públicas Para el Equidad y el Crecimiento, Argentina

Like CDD in Ghana, the Center for the Implementation of Public Policies Promoting Equity and Growth (Centro de Implementación de Políticas Públicas Para el Equidad y el Crecimiento, CIPPEC) examined the loss of scarce education resources to teacher absenteeism and school closures.[10] In addition, CIPPEC analysts calculated the monetary value of these lost resources. They suspected that absenteeism and school closures disproportionately affect poorer areas and that, once accounted for, poorer students effectively receive fewer education resources than do wealthier students.

This suspicion turned out to be correct. CIPPEC analysts collected absenteeism data for 31 high schools in two Buenos Aires districts—Florencio Varela, which is poorer than average, and San Martín, which is wealthier. The analysts interviewed principals and reviewed teacher attendance records from October and June, two school months without vacations or exams.[11] Analysts counted each time a teacher was marked absent in teacher records for randomly selected courses; absences due to closure of the entire school were marked "school closures."[12] This distinction allowed CIPPEC to measure the effects of individual absenteeism independent of school closures. The team calculated the monetary value of each class hour lost to absenteeism and confirmed that, because of lost class time, poorer schools receive far fewer resources.

Class time lost

CIPPEC found that absenteeism and school closures cost Argentine students a tremendous amount of class time.[13] On average across the surveyed schools, teacher absenteeism cost schools 12.3 hours of class time a month, or 11.5 percent of the 107.1 hours of mandated class time. Another 15.1 hours a month, or 14 percent of class time, were lost to school closures—the results of strikes, teacher conferences, facility problems (such as lack of heat), and other reasons. Together these represent an average loss of 5.5 days a month—or 49 days out of the 180 day school year. Students lost this class time even though there is a legal requirement that a substitute teacher or some other alternative be provided when the primary teacher is absent.[14]

The severity of the problem was far from uniform across schools or time. In both October and June one school lost less than 10 hours on average, while four schools lost more than 40 hours, including one school that lost 47.2 hours. In that school 60 percent of the loss was due to school closings and 40 percent to absenteeism, while in two other schools 80 percent of the loss was due to absenteeism. In two schools teacher absenteeism averaged more than 20 hours between the two months; nine of the thirty-one schools lost more than 15 hours just to absenteeism. Likewise, while some schools had minimal closures, nine schools lost more than 20 hours a month and one lost 35 hours.

Analysts found that the severity of the problem also varied between the two districts. On average, Florencio Varela, the poorer district, lost more class time to teacher absenteeism and school closure in both October and June than did San Martín, the wealthier district. In October schools in San Martín missed only half as many days as schools in Florencio Varela. On average, students in Florencio Varela were deprived of nearly a third of all classes, while those in San Martín missed less than a fifth (figure 4.2).

To calculate the difference between the education resources received by schools in the two districts, CIPPEC analysts compared the monthly value of the class hours each student should receive with the hours actually received for each district. First, analysts calculated the budgetary value of a single class hour, AR$33.3, by dividing the schools' per teacher personnel expenditures by the total number of hours included in the 2007 budget.[15] Second, they multiplied this hourly value by the number of hours of class time a student should receive according to the province curriculum, which provided a reference value for a month of class time in Buenos Aires high schools: AR$3,589. By subtracting the value of the lost hours in each school, the analysts calculated the "effective expenditure." The shortfall, or difference between full expenditure and effective expenditure, varied considerably across schools—in some schools it was just 4–5 percent, while in one it was as high as 64.4 percent (table 4.3). Averaging the shortfalls in the two districts shows that Florencio Varela—the poorer district that lost more class time to absenteeism and

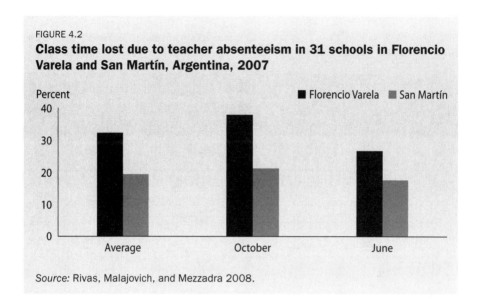

FIGURE 4.2

Class time lost due to teacher absenteeism in 31 schools in Florencio Varela and San Martín, Argentina, 2007

Source: Rivas, Malajovich, and Mezzadra 2008.

school closures—had a shortfall of AR$1,165 a month, 40 percent more than that of San Martín, the wealthier district, which had a shortfall of AR$693.

Causes of absenteeism

CIPPEC analysts also wanted to understand what was behind the high rates of teacher absenteeism and school closure in its 31 schools. They first analyzed absenteeism data from the Directorate General of Culture and Education of the Province of Buenos Aires[16] and found that the most common reason for absenteeism was the same one found by CDD in Ghana: illness. Some 40 percent of teacher absences were related to personal illness, and 14 percent were because of a family member's illness or another personal reason. Some 9 percent were due to exams or other leave, including marriage and noncovered maternity leave, and 4 percent were due to teacher strikes, though not strikes that closed the entire school (which would have counted as school closures). In 18 percent of cases the cause of the absence is unknown because the school did not inform the directorate. Although most absences were for personal reasons, CIPPEC found that an average of 9 percent of lost class time was due to school administration, such as supervisors assigning teachers to department meetings, interschool activities, or administrative duties. Additionally, schools sometimes closed because authorities organized teacher conferences.

Like CDD, when CIPPEC analysts looked at the distribution of absenteeism throughout the week, they found that most occurred toward the end of the week.

TABLE 4.3

Shortfall due to lost class hours in 31 schools in Florencio Varela and San Martín, Argentina, 2007

School	Effective expenditure (AR$)		Shortfall from full expenditure (AR$)		Shortfall as a share of full expenditure (percent)	
	June	October	June	October	June	October
1	2,646.3	3,559.6	771.7	200.3	22.6	5.3
2	2,333.9	2,371.3	1,084.2	1,388.6	31.7	36.9
3	2,675.7	1,825.2	742.4	1,934.7	21.7	51.5
4	2,608.9	2,646.3	809.1	1,113.5	23.7	29.6
5	2,345.9	1,683.6	1,072.1	2,076.2	31.4	55.2
6	2,813.2	2,379.3	604.8	1,380.6	17.7	36.7
7	2,546.2	2,646.3	871.9	1,113.5	25.5	29.6
8	2,200.4	2,004.1	1,217.7	1,755.7	35.6	46.7
9	2,746.4	2,742.4	671.6	1,017.4	19.6	27.1
10	2,241.7	2,337.9	1,176.3	1,422.0	34.4	37.8
11	2,813.2	1,337.8	604.8	2,422.0	17.7	64.4
12	2,237.7	2,155.0	1,180.3	1,604.9	34.5	42.7
13	2,980.1	2,604.9	437.9	1,154.9	12.8	30.7
14	2,200.4	2,442.0	1,217.7	1,317.8	35.6	35.0
15	3,247.1	3,288.5	170.9	471.3	5.0	12.5
16	2,471.4	2,738.4	946.6	1,021.4	27.7	27.2
17	2,946.7	2,471.4	471.3	1,288.4	13.8	34.3
18	2,504.8	3,080.2	913.3	679.6	26.7	18.1
19	2,263.1	2,404.6	1,154.9	1,355.2	33.8	36.0
20	3,217.8	3,251.1	200.3	508.7	5.9	13.5
21	2,950.7	3,046.9	467.3	713.0	13.7	19.0
22	2,980.1	2,909.3	437.9	850.5	12.8	22.6
23	2,805.2	3,050.9	612.8	709.0	17.9	18.9
24	2,913.3	2,884.0	504.7	875.9	14.8	23.3
25	2,980.1	2,842.6	437.9	917.3	12.8	24.4
26	2,713.1	3,592.9	705.0	166.9	20.6	4.4
27	2,813.2	2,612.9	604.8	1,146.9	17.7	30.5
28	2,779.8	3,046.9	638.2	713.0	18.7	19.0
29	3,046.9	2,984.1	371.2	775.7	10.9	20.6
30	—	—	—	—	—	—
31	2,642.3	3,180.4	775.7	579.5	22.7	15.4
Average	2,688.9	2,670.7	729.2	1,089.1	21.3	29.0

— is unavailable.

Source: Rivas, Malajovich, and Mezzadra 2008.

In June, a month without teacher strikes, there were 390 registered absences, 12 percent of them on Monday, 18–20 percent each day from Tuesday–Thursday, and 31 percent on Friday.

CIPPEC analysts also gleaned insights from interviews.[17] Interviewees cited both insufficient state support for teachers in difficult and tiring jobs and a lack of control in the education system that permits teachers to abuse their labor rights as reasons for absenteeism. All but one of the principals interviewed by CIPPEC agreed that absenteeism disrupted school, angered parents, and exhausted students. Several quotes collected by CIPPEC from interviews with principals illustrate their sentiments:

- "No teacher is capable of confronting the psychological, social, and behavioral problems of students. There is a general saturation. Even those who have been committed to their work for years are fed up."
- "The professors are worn out. The work in a school like this is exhausting. You have to be here to understand it."
- "Last week I had to request a substitute in the morning for Contemporary Culture and Art. When the teacher showed up, it was a teacher who had already taken the day off sick. This isn't ethical."
- "They go so far as bringing in fake doctors' notes. Once I became aware of this I reported it to the supervisor, but they told me there is nothing that can be done. The only thing left to do is go through the courts."
- "Before you couldn't leave your house if you asked for sick leave, but now, no one controls it. The math professor who was supposedly sick, the director found her perfectly relaxed on San Bernardo beach."
- "The problem is that any doctor can give you a note. Before it wasn't like that, you had to go to the Delegation of Medical Examiners, and there was more control. Since they closed the Delegation in San Martín, absenteeism has skyrocketed."

CIPPEC's interviews uncovered few efforts to mitigate or make up for teacher absenteeism. The interviews revealed that principals rarely try to curb absenteeism, either formally or informally. Yet the strategies of principals who do try are instructive. One principal distributed a statistical analysis of teacher absenteeism among her staff to increase awareness of the problem. In another school, where teacher tardiness was a problem, late teachers were docked a half-hour's pay, which, according to the principal, improved punctuality. But one prefect related that the principal at his school had tried marking down repeatedly absent teachers on their annual evaluations but, under pressure from the union, eventually gave maximum scores to all teachers.

The interviews also suggest that schools rarely make up for teacher absenteeism, either with substitute teachers or by other strategies. When asked about strategies to ameliorate absenteeism, only 1 percent of the respondents reported using officially assigned substitutes.[18] Most respondents (61 percent) said that they filled the time with either supervised or unsupervised free class time or by having the students leave early or arrive late. In other cases the time was filled with cultural activities such as movies or sports (15 percent) or schoolwork assigned by the absent teacher (11 percent).[19] The inescapable conclusion of CIPPEC's analysis is that the time students lose to teacher absenteeism is rarely recovered.

Causes of school closures

Closure of entire schools was just as pervasive and cost students more class time than teacher absenteeism did. During October, 28 of the 31 schools CIPPEC studied missed at least one day of class because the school was closed.

Analysts discovered that the primary cause of these closures depended on the month. Closures in October were due primarily to a large number of teacher strikes—each averaging three days and totaling 24 closures. Closures in June were due primarily to teacher conferences, which caused 19 closures. Another reason for a closure was lack of basic services (such as heat or electricity), which caused five closures in June and three in October. And a large number of closures—on average 19 each month—were due to other factors—extreme rain, for example, or elections.[20]

More surprising, CIPPEC interviews with principals showed that many begin the school year without enough teachers, which causes a substantial amount of lost class time. Some 55 percent of principals said that their school had unfilled teaching positions for one or more subjects at the start of the year, which caused students to lose between two weeks and two months of class time for that subject. Yet even when the vacancy remained for months, classes were never taught by officially assigned substitutes, and the school principal assigned an alternate substitute in only 12 percent of cases. Here, too, analysts found the problem more pronounced in the poorer district: an astounding 64 percent of the schools in Florencio Varela had at least one unfilled teaching position at the start of the year, compared with 47 percent of schools in San Martín.

Responses to the vacancies also differed between the two districts. In Florencio Varela the primary solution to teacher vacancies was to allow students to arrive late or leave early (67 percent), while the most common solution in San Martín was to give students a supervised free period (44 percent). Some 25 percent of the principals in San Martín said they had assigned substitutes themselves (informally, not officially assigned substitutes), and 13 percent said that in lieu of class they had instead involved students in cultural activities. In Florencio Varela no principals assigned informal substitutes or involved the students in cultural activities.

Likewise, only one school was found to have recovered school days lost to closures. Thus with school closures, as with absenteeism, the hours students miss are never recovered.

As with CDD in Ghana, CIPPEC's analysis demonstrates how an independent monitoring organization can leverage its understanding of the education system to develop original insights into a particularly intransigent problem. CIPPEC's conclusions, like CDD's, are about specific local areas and do not necessarily generalize nationally. But at the very least they hint at broader dynamics reducing the effectiveness of education in Argentina, especially for students in poorer districts, where teacher absenteeism and school closures seem far more prevalent. CIPPEC also illustrates another potential advantage to independent monitoring organizations' work: unlike CDD, which worked separately from the government, CIPPEC undertook its analysis with the blessing and cooperation of the Ministry of Education, with which it had worked many times in the past and whose staff was surprised by the findings and interested in developing solutions (see chapter 5).

Institute of Policy Analysis and Research, Kenya

The Institute of Policy Analysis and Research (IPAR) in Nairobi, Kenya, conducted a study on education that is discussed in chapter 3, but another team undertook a separate study on absenteeism in Kenyan healthcare.[21] Salaries in Kenya's public health system are lower than those in the private sector, and there is little flexibility in the pay scale for performance—workers are paid according to their seniority and education level, not their commitment or effectiveness on the job. Healthcare professionals are rarely disciplined for repeated absences, and the most common sanction is a transfer to an undesirable location. Thus professionals in the public healthcare system, especially the best and the brightest, may be strongly tempted to skip work to moonlight in the private sector.[22] IPAR examined absenteeism at 40 health facilities of different types in Machakos, a mixed urban-rural district in Kenya's Eastern province. Unannounced visits by the IPAR team recorded an average absenteeism rate of 25 percent. Analysts estimated that if this rate were repeated across the year, these absences would cost the government KES 6,659,832 (about $85,000) a month, for just that one district.

Absenteeism is widespread

IPAR staff made two unannounced visits, one at 8:30 am and one at 2:00 pm, to the 40 facilities in its study—the district hospital, three subdistrict hospitals, 15 health centers, and 21 dispensaries—to check whether more than 400 full-time staff members had shown up for work. Each staff member was classified as "present," "absent half-day," or "absent all day."[23] On average, about 25 percent of workers were absent, and the absenteeism rates from the morning and afternoon checks were nearly identical.

The results were far from identical across professions (table 4.4). The workers most likely to be absent were skilled technical workers—those who would have the best private sector prospects. Pharmacists had the highest absenteeism rate (41.6 percent), followed by laboratory technicians (39.1 percent), and doctors (28.5 percent). Nurses, who comprise more than half the full-time staff that IPAR checked for, were absent much less (18.9 percent). The least likely to be absent were public health staff (13 percent).

Absenteeism is clearly endemic in this sample, but analysts note that the results should not be wholly surprising, given skilled healthcare workers' temptation to supplement their income in the private sector. Healthcare professionals have the chance to earn high fees seeing patients privately or working in private clinics or pharmacies. And, as mentioned, they generally face few penalties for missing work. In fact, they remain valued by public facilities that recognize that they cannot pay wages and benefits commensurate with the private sector. For example, a 2006 attempt to force medical doctors to work for eight hours a day was met with stiff resistance, and the proposal was eventually abandoned. In fact, of those who were absent during IPAR analysts' checks, about half had official permission to be absent: 12.6 percent were on official leave, and 7.4 percent were on sick time. Another 7.6 percent were absent because of official duties elsewhere, even though these absences sometimes meant that vital services were unavailable. For

TABLE 4.4

Recorded absences of key public healthcare staff in Machakos District, Kenya, 2008

Profession	Total staff	Number of staff that analysts checked on	Absence rate (percent)
Pharmacists	32	12	41.6
Laboratory technicians	55	22	39.1
Medical doctors	58	53	28.5
Clinical officers	64	48	21.5
Nurses	548	270	18.9
Public health staff	40	12	13.0

Source: Muthama and others 2008.

example, one facility's laboratory was completely closed because the lab technician was attending a workshop. And 16.2 percent of absent workers were reported to be "off duty," which analysts discovered is an informal arrangement developed among workers, usually nurses, by which they decided who could miss work on a given day.

Explaining absenteeism

IPAR analysts dug more deeply into these results to identify individual-level factors that might make a worker more likely to miss work. Analysts interviewed a sample of workers about the number of days and hours they had been absent in the previous three months as well as about their demographic characteristics, job satisfaction, financial and personal stress, and the ambiguity or clarity of their role at work. Analysts also noted the characteristics of these employees' facilities, such as wages, whether housing was provided, and remoteness. They then checked for correlations between these data and employees' reported absenteeism over the last month.[24]

Many of these factors showed no correlation with the number of hours that employees reported being absent. But lower absenteeism rates were associated with workers who have worked at a facility for a long time—perhaps because they have developed a sense of commitment to their patients—and with workers who live at their facility (the average staff member living onsite reported being absent for 46 hours over the preceding three months, compared with 73 hours for those living offsite). Higher absenteeism was correlated with workers who earn more—which fits the previous section's findings that doctors and pharmacists are absent more often. Likewise, workers in rural facilities were absent less than urban workers—55 hours, on average, over the preceding three months, compared with 84 hours for urban workers—which may reflect the greater earning potential in the private sector in urban areas.

Those who reported job-related stress were absent more, and those who were satisfied with their jobs were absent less: 23 percent of those who said they were satisfied reported being absent in the preceding three months, compared with 37 percent of those who said they were not satisfied. Married staff were absent much more often (77 hours) than unmarried staff (39 hours).

The cost of absenteeism

IPAR wanted to get a rough sense of how much absenteeism was costing the government—that is, how much the government was paying for work that was not done because the worker was absent. Analysts assumed that the absenteeism rates they found were a good proxy for absenteeism generally for that profession in the Machakos district. They then calculated an average monthly wage for workers in each profession and multiplied that wage by the profession's absenteeism rate (table 4.5).

IPAR calculated that this absenteeism costs the Kenyan government KES 6,659,832 ($85,000) a month in wasted resources for this district—or a little over $1 million a year. Though nurses have a relatively low rate of absenteeism, they account for almost half the waste because there are so many of them. Doctors and pharmacists follow. Even though there are fewer of them, they earn high salaries and are often absent.

These are rough estimates: salaries differ for workers in the same profession, and IPAR's estimates of absenteeism may not be valid for the whole district over an entire month. Other absenteeism studies in this chapter found substantial differences in absenteeism across the week; there is no way to know whether absenteeism was higher or lower than average on the day IPAR did its research. Nonetheless, IPAR's estimates do suggest that absenteeism squanders an appalling amount of Kenya's scarce healthcare resources.

El Centro de Investigaciones Económicas Nacionales, Guatemala

Guatemala's National Center for Economic Research (Centro de Investigaciones Económicas Nacionales CIEN) evaluated six government programs aimed at getting poorer students to go to and stay in school.[25] The programs are designed to

TABLE 4.5

Resources wasted by absenteeism among public healthcare staff in Machakos District, Kenya, 2008

Profession	Absence rate (percent)	Total staff	Average salary (KES per month)	Resources wasted due to absenteeism (KES per month)
Pharmacists	41.6	32	86,000	1,144,832
Laboratory technicians[a]	39.1	55	30,286	651,300
Medical doctors	28.5	53	86,000	1,151,970
Clinical officers	21.5	64	30,286	416,736
Nurses	18.9	548	30,286	3,136,781
Public health staff	13.0	40	30,286	157,487
Total		792		6,659,832

a. Includes laboratory technicians and technologists.
Source: Muthama and others 2008.

both lower the cost of attending school and raise the value, or quality, of education. Analysts uncovered several problems with the programs, notably that funding is inadequate and that resources usually arrive late. But CIEN also found that program benefits are equitably distributed—at least between urban and rural schools—and that satisfaction among beneficiaries is very high. The results thus suggest ways to make six successful programs even more successful—which naturally appealed to the Guatemalan government. In fact, chapter 6 shows that the government responded very positively to the findings and is already making adjustments to correct some of the problems CIEN uncovered.

Five of the government programs that CIEN evaluated aim to lower the cost of education by providing scholarships, textbooks, supplies, and meals and milk at school. One aimed to increase education quality by providing teachers with supplies. To check the efficiency and effectiveness of spending on these six programs, CIEN analysts selected 41 schools—20 urban and 21 rural—from the 715 in the *departamento* of Guatemala, the region that includes the capital, Guatemala City.[26] Survey staff interviewed students, teachers, parents, and school board members about their experiences with the government programs: whether funding arrived on time, was adequate, reached its intended beneficiaries, and was equitable between rural and urban students.

Funding is inadequate . . .

The first problem analysts uncovered is that funding is simply inadequate (table 4.6). Some students receive supplies for only part of the year, and some are provided meals or milk only on some days. Of the six programs, only funding for the textbook program appears to be even close to adequate.

The programs that provide meals and milk appeared to have the worst funding shortfall. While 97 percent of head teachers reported receiving funding to provide meals, and 90 percent said they gave meals to every student in their school, only 27 percent of school board members said that the resources provided were sufficient to feed all students. Schools appear to be compensating for insufficient funding by not feeding students every day. Head teachers and students both report that meals were served an average of four days a week; in some schools students reported receiving meals just one day a week. The milk program, which supplements the meals program by providing students a glass of milk with each meal, appeared to have even more trouble meeting needs. Only 28 percent of head teachers reported that all children received a glass of milk in 2008. Some 68 percent of students said that they received milk five days a week, 11 percent said they received milk only two days a week, and 8 percent said they received milk just one day a week.

TABLE 4.6
Adequacy of resources for six Guatemala education programs, 2008

Program	Adequacy of resources	General results
School supplies	39 percent of head teachers reported receiving just enough resources, 58 percent reported receiving not enough.	More than half of head teachers report receiving insufficient resources in 2008.
Textbooks	Roughly half of head teachers reported that not enough textbooks were distributed.[a]	Budget allocation is high enough that textbooks were distributed in 95 percent of the schools in 2008. However, head teachers report that textbooks were rarely enough to meet the needs of all grades.
School meals	97 percent of head teachers acknowledge receipt of resources under the school meals program, but only 27 percent of school board members reported that resources were enough to provide meals to all children.	School board members may not think resources are sufficient because the resources may not be enough to provide meals all days of the week (the average is four days).
Milk	73 percent of head teachers report that they received just enough milk, 18 percent that there was not enough, and 9 percent that there was more than enough.	Only 28 percent of schools are implementing the milk program. Students state that they get milk on average four times a week.[b]
Teaching kit	82 percent of teachers reported receiving the teaching kit; 97 percent of head teachers reported receiving one.	Head teachers seem to benefit to a greater extent than teachers from the program.
Scholarship	No questions asked.	Not evaluated.

a. Percentage of teachers who reported not receiving enough textbooks for each grade: grade 1, 49 percent; grade 2, 51 percent; grade 3, 43 percent; grade 4, 51 percent; grade 5, 54 percent; grade 6, 54 percent.

b. Direct observation by survey staff suggested that 64 percent of schools were distributing milk on the day of the survey.

Source: Cuevas and Lavarreda 2008.

The programs that provide supplies—school supplies to students and teaching kits to teachers—fared better but still had funding problems. More than half of head teachers—58 percent—reported that they were not provided sufficient resources to purchase supplies in 2008 (a higher proportion than in 2007[27]). And 24 percent of students reported that the supplies they received in 2007 did not last them through the year; 90 percent of them said that their parents paid for some supplies, and the remaining 10 percent went without supplies. As for the teaching kits, 82 percent of surveyed teachers said they had received one in 2008—though the mix of supplies varied widely and was often inadequate. For example, half of surveyed teachers reported receiving pencils and dry erase markers in 2008, but only 2 of the 283 teachers reported receiving maps. Head teachers seemed more likely to have received kits than regular teachers did: 97 percent of those surveyed said they had received one.

Analysts found a smaller funding shortfall in the textbook program. Nearly all head teachers said they received textbooks in 2008 (95 percent, down slightly from 97 percent in 2007). But in all six grades, 43–54 percent of head teachers reported that the textbooks they received were not sufficient; 54 percent asked parents to purchase additional textbooks.

Only 12 of 432 parents surveyed reported qualifying for the scholarship program. But this low proportion may not signal insufficient funding because the program is targeted at very poor families, and the area around the schools studied has a lower poverty rate than elsewhere in Guatemala.

In part, these resource insufficiencies may be due to poor spending decisions. For example, many schools appear to be purchasing goods at high prices. Using invoices provided by school boards for purchases of 18 goods—such as paper, notepads, scissors, and glue—analysts calculated that schools could have saved 21 percent of the Q954,665 (about $126,000) spent on school supplies by purchasing the supplies at the lowest available price. Overpaying for food may have wasted even more: up to 30 percent of the resources allocated for meals.[28]

... and resources arrive late

Analysts also found that funding and resources rarely arrive when they should (figure 4.3).[29] Especially hard hit are the programs that provide supplies and textbooks. Just 28 percent of students reported getting textbooks in January 2008, when school started. Distribution in the supplies program was worse. Only 7 percent of students said they had received supplies in January 2008. Some 53 percent of students said they did not receive their supplies until April, although by May only 10 percent lacked supplies.

Fewer delays were reported with the food programs. Just 33 percent of students reported that they started receiving meals in January 2008, but by March more than 90 percent were receiving meals. The milk program, which covers fewer students, showed a similar pattern: only 16 percent of students reported that they started to get a glass of milk with their school meal in January 2008; by March it had reached nearly 40 percent of students, more than the number eligible.[30]

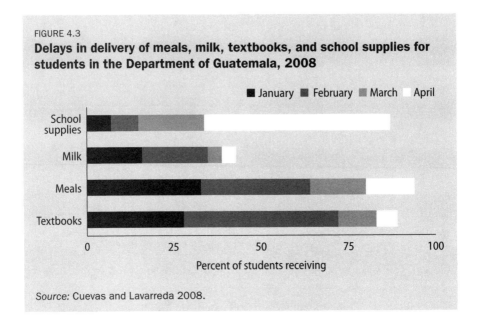

FIGURE 4.3

Delays in delivery of meals, milk, textbooks, and school supplies for students in the Department of Guatemala, 2008

■ January ■ February ■ March □ April

Percent of students receiving

Source: Cuevas and Lavarreda 2008.

CIEN also found delays in the scholarship program. Only 12 of 432 parents surveyed reported that a child in their family was eligible for a scholarship, but just 1 of them reported receiving the scholarship in January. CIEN did not examine the timeliness of the teaching kit program.

Rural and urban schools both benefit from the programs . . .

There were bright spots in CIEN's analysis. First, it turns out that rural schools, which are in poorer areas, do actually benefit more from these programs, which were designed to target them. In 2008, 96 percent of the teachers in rural schools reported receiving school supplies, compared with 83 percent of urban teachers, and 92 percent of rural teachers reported receiving teaching kits, compared with 72 percent of urban teachers. Rural schools also had slightly higher allocations of funding for school meals and milk. Students from rural schools reported receiving an average of 4.5 meals a week, whereas students from urban schools reported receiving an average of 3.6 meals a week. Rural students reported receiving milk 4.4 times a week, urban students 3.8 times a week.

. . . and satisfaction with the programs is high

The second bright spot is that satisfaction among program beneficiaries was high. For example, 96 percent of surveyed students said that they were satisfied with the food served under the school meals program.[31] And 91 percent of head teachers who participated in the milk program said they were satisfied with it and believed that it met its objectives; 90 percent of students who received milk liked it, and 96 percent of them said they were getting enough. Head teachers did report a few problems with the milk program—27 percent said they received sour milk, and 9 percent reported that their milk soured while in storage at school.

Satisfaction is also high with the supplies programs: 72 percent of head teachers who received school supplies reported being satisfied with the school supplies program and believed that the program meets its objectives. Similar levels of satisfaction were registered for the teacher kit program: 79 percent of head teachers claimed to be satisfied, and 77 percent thought that the program's objectives were being met. The lowest satisfaction among head teachers was with the textbooks program: only 44 percent said the program was fully meeting its objectives. Yet two-thirds still said they were satisfied with it, and 92 percent said the textbooks provided are used. And 86 percent of students said they were satisfied with the textbooks.

In short, the problems that CIEN found had less to do with implementation than with the timing and adequacy of resources. The results suggest that if the delays could be reduced, six fairly successful government programs would work even better. Chapter 6 shows that the Guatemalan government was receptive to CIEN's findings and has begun taking steps to deal with the delays.

Gdansk Institute of Market Economics, Poland

The Gdansk Institute of Market Economics (GIME) in Poland conducted two studies as part of the Transparency and Accountability Project.[32] As the Soviet Union collapsed, the first item on virtually every country's agenda was to decentralize. They had had enough of centralization. Almost every newly independent government shifted ownership of primary and secondary schools, as well as hospitals and health clinics, to local governments. Ownership of the larger units tended to move to regional or provincial governments, and smaller units to counties or municipalities.

These changes were made just as the economies collapsed, so ownership was often shifted without adequate funding. Moreover, the Soviet Union invested heavily in infrastructure, so when the costs of operating the facilities shifted to market prices, the economic burden of the infrastructure was overwhelming. Further complicated by shrinking populations, every country is still struggling with solutions 20 years on.

GIME's first study examined the impact of central transfers to regions and localities to finance education and health. After reviewing information about poverty in Poland and concluding that poverty is primarily a rural phenomenon, GIME narrowed the question to ask how well the funding streams from the central government offset the inability of poorer local governments to subsidize services with their own money.

For primary and secondary education GIME concluded that most of the existing transfer mechanism from the center was unnecessary. Urban areas could fully finance schools with their own resources, and poor rural areas did not get enough money through the existing formula to finance their schools, in part because of higher costs in less dense settings. GIME argued for a shift to a simple equalization grant to be sure all localities could provide the same level of education to their children.

For health GIME found that in rural areas, where costs of delivering care are higher and people are fewer, the capitation payment used to finance primary care was inadequate. GIME also found that circumstances differed so much across communities that the family doctor model in which each Polish citizen signs up with a provider did not work well in many situations. GIME recommended that localities be given the option to organize primary care in the way they want rather than to have the entire country follow the same model.

For hospitals GIME documented a disastrous combination of an implicit guarantee of debts by local governments and poor accountability of hospital managers that led to heavy reliance on debt financing—to suppliers, employees, and governments (for example, for payroll taxes)—to supplement operating budgets. GIME was concerned that the level of debt could bankrupt not only the hospitals but also local governments and that previous programs to eliminate it had not succeeded. GIME argued that any future program to solve the debt problem would require the equivalent of a bankruptcy procedure to change the hospital management (to make managers accountable) and put the hospital on a road to self-financing.

The second study was intended to be an application of a Public Expenditure Tracking Survey focusing on the hospital debt problem to understand in detail why it happened and what a permanent solution might look like. Hospital debts have been a problem in Poland since hospitals became autonomous in 1998 and were required to finance all operations through service provision. Nearly all services are paid for by the National Health Fund, which covers almost the entire population. Local governments are not allowed to provide operating subsidies, but they can finance capital improvements because they are the owners. Many local governments provide loans for operating costs, but these have to be booked as debt and paid back. By 2006 hospitals had accumulated about PLN 10 billion of debt, about 40 percent of the National Health Fund's annual revenue.

In responding to the Transparency and Accountability Project's request for proposals, GIME originally planned to visit a sample of hospitals, tally their accounts, and interview administrators and other key informants. The analysts subsequently discovered that they could access a database of financial filings by the hospitals that would allow them to more efficiently and robustly analyze the hospitals' finances. So instead of the original research plan, they analyzed the data, picked four hospitals to visit, and wrote up detailed case studies of them.[33] This strategy produced an impressive report that appeals to both those who are convinced by numbers and those who are convinced by stories or examples.

The database covered 491 public general hospitals organized as "self-financing public healthcare facilities," or 78 percent of public hospitals. The first finding was that between 2004 and 2006, 24 percent of the hospitals had no debt, 63 percent had declining debt, and 13 percent had increasing debt. Further analysis showed that 20 percent of the hospitals accounted for 47 percent of the debt by 2006, and 20 percent accounted for 78 percent of the "matured debt" or past due bills. Indebted hospitals generally blamed their situation on revenue falling short of the costs of providing patient services—in other words, the National Health Fund was not reimbursing for actual costs. GIME analysts used the wide range of experience in hospitals' debt management to try to understand whether this was in fact the case. They concluded that National Health Fund reimbursement was adequate, as statistically similar hospitals had completely different experiences with debt. Hospitals became indebted because they were much worse at managing their costs, primarily their payroll costs.

The four case studies examined hospitals with different records of restructuring and cost management. Each successful restructuring among them involved slashing personnel expenses, which GIME found consistent with its quantitative findings. To be able to reduce employment, authorities needed to let the situation become a crisis. Without a crisis they could not make the changes needed because of public opposition, especially among employees and their allies. One hospital that restructured itself into a private company (owned by the municipality) went from 325 staff to 200 overnight. The original 11 surgeons were reduced to 4, who nearly doubled the volume of surgeries. The detailed work confirmed GIME's suspicions based on the first study: that incentives needed to be aligned for hospital managers to reduce debt and eliminate it as a way to finance daily operations. Chapter 6 discusses their recommendations and changes in policy in Poland.

Conclusion

After money is allocated and distributed, it is spent. This is where the rubber meets the road, where one can see whether resources are improving lives. The connection between resources and service delivery is hardly automatic. Resources may not be adequate to deliver a sufficient volume of quality services or could be used in a way that means that certain citizens receive more benefit than others. Resources also may simply be wasted, used to pay the salaries of service providers like teachers and nurses who fail to show up to work.

Exploring the links between resources and effective service delivery is a task at which independent monitoring organizations truly excel. The organizations highlighted in this chapter asked simple questions—whether teachers were teaching, whether resources were sufficient and arrived on time, and whether intended beneficiaries were satisfied. Yet answering such questions was far from elementary. It required knowledge of what programs or spending patterns would illustrate a government's performance in delivering services or where resources should be going in the first place. It required knowing when schools or clinics should be visited to gauge absenteeism, why teachers or healthcare workers might be absent, and what third-party information could be used to cross-check results. The analysts whose work is highlighted in this chapter had a leg up on these issues simply by living day-to-day with the government and its services. Each was able to uncover important problems with service delivery. And because they live with the services, each is now able to keep a constant watch on them, to see if the problems persist.

This chapter completes the discussion of how independent monitoring organizations study service delivery. Chapter 2 demonstrated some of the benefits of an independent monitoring organization's simply trying to gather the relevant data on a chosen government service priority or program of local importance, which in itself can offer important insights into government transparency and performance. Chapter 3 showed how several independent monitoring organizations were able to demystify the most opaque resource flows. This chapter rounds out the picture, providing examples of extensive efforts by independent monitoring organizations to understand how well resources are translated into services.

But studying spending and service delivery is—or should be—only the start. Each of these organizations set out not just to find problems but also to formulate remedies and constructively disseminate them and the analysis supporting them. Their analysis was a tool with a purpose—better policies or services. For independent monitoring organizations these steps are especially important, because for them a service delivery problem is not abstract; it affects their daily lives. Chapters 5 and 6 turn to independent monitoring organizations' efforts to use what they have learned to improve service delivery.

Notes

1. Spending data are in terms of purchasing power parity to better reflect what $1 actually buys in Ghana. The values would be even lower if the exchange rate were used. See Griffin (2009).

2. For example, a 2007 report found that Ghanaian students spend less than half the officially mandated amount of time in class and that teacher absenteeism was a major cause (Abadzi 2007).

3. Gyimah-Boadi and others 2008.

4. The research team designed separate surveys for teachers and head teachers. The surveys were written by CDD, but some of the questions were drawn from similar surveys in Bangladesh and Uganda.

5. Analysts used a multistage stratified random sampling procedure to ensure that the sample included schools in varied locations. For the first level of stratification the country was divided into three broad zones: northern, central, and southern. One region was randomly selected per zone. Then one district was randomly chosen in each region. The selected districts were Wa West in the Upper West Region, Asante Akim North in the Ashanti Region, and Birim North in the Eastern Region. The research team wanted the sample to reflect the distribution of schools in each district. They first categorized the schools in each district as rural or urban, using lists of public primary schools available from the district education directorates. They then selected schools randomly so that the sample reflected the actual division of schools in the district between urban and rural. For example, the probability of a rural school's selection was proportional to the number of schools in the district that were rural. Since the majority of schools in the districts were rural, the analysts ended with a sample that was 82 percent rural and 18 percent urban.

6. Upon arrival in each school, the team met with the head teacher, or the teacher in charge if the head teacher was absent, and interviewed the teachers and the head teacher one-on-one. The questionnaire for the head teachers gathered a list of every teacher in the school, their qualifications, and whether they were present that day. After the interviews, the analysts who interviewed the head teacher then checked with colleagues who interviewed the individual teachers to ensure that those who were reported absent were physically absent. Teachers on leave or suspension were excluded from the list. These visits covered both morning and afternoon periods, with most schools receiving at least two visits during the week. The team also requested and made copies of teacher attendance logs whenever they were available.

7. CDD also compared absenteeism across the three districts. The highest teacher absence was in Birim North, with more than half (56 percent) of teachers absent during at least one of the visits, followed by Asante Akim North (43 percent) and Wa West (42 percent).

But the frequency of absence was highest in Wa West, with 19 percent of teachers absent at least twice, compared with 15 percent each in Asante Akim North and Birim North.

8. CDD analysts recorded the physical facilities available at each school, including, among others, the presence of a staff common room, access to potable water, and the presence of a playground and pupils' desks, as well as proximity to services such as banks, bus or truck stations, and health centers. Except for playgrounds, most schools lacked basic facilities such as potable water, electricity, and pupils' desks. Half even lacked teachers' desks.

9. In all, CDD researchers interviewed 134 teachers (87 male and 47 female) and 28 head teachers (26 male and 2 female). The team also gathered qualitative data on teacher absenteeism from focus group discussions with the leadership of parent–teacher associations and school management committees, which are school management bodies that oversee the day-to-day administration.

10. Rivas, Malajovich, and Mezzadra 2008.

11. CIPPEC conducted its study in the *conurbano* of Buenos Aires, a ring of 24 urban districts around the city that are home to more than 60 percent of the total population of the province of Buenos Aires and that experience higher rates of poverty than the city of Buenos Aires (30 percent of the *conurbano* population lives below the poverty line, compared with 10 percent of the city population, based on data from the Census and the Permanent Household Survey [Encuesta Permanente de Hogares] from the National Institute of Statistics). CIPPEC conducted fieldwork in high schools (grades 10–12) in two *conurbano* districts. To test the hypothesis that effective spending varies with the district's socioeconomic status, CIPPEC chose districts with varying socioeconomic profiles: Florencio Varela has a high percentage of households with unmet basic needs (27 percent), and San Martín has a low percentage of households with unmet basic needs (11 percent); the average share of households with unmet basic needs for the province of Buenos Aires was 13 percent. INDEC (1984) defines households with unmet basic needs as those with at least one of the following indicators of deprivation: overcrowding (more than three people per room), housing (unsuitable home: tenancy bedroom, precariously built home, or other type), sanitary conditions (no type of toilet), pressure on head of household (four or more people per bread winner), and a head of household with low education achievement (two or fewer years of primary school).

12. Teachers were considered absent when they did not teach their assigned class or classes on a day the school was open, regardless of the reason. Thus, general strikes when the entire school was closed were considered school closures, but teachers who participated independently in a strike that did not close the school were considered absent. Likewise, teacher conferences that occupied the entire school were considered closures,

but teachers who were sent to meetings or conferences by school administrators were considered absent.

13. And since CIPPEC used official records, their results are likely underestimated.

14. Since CIPPEC analysts focused on lost class time, they considered only instances of teacher absence for which the school did not provide a substitute; they did not consider absenteeism in which the teacher was absent but a substitute teacher was provided. In fact, schools very rarely used substitute teachers.

15. Directorate General of Education and Culture of the Province of Buenos Aires 2007.

16. In Argentina students remain in one classroom, while teachers rotate. Teachers must sign a document to verify their presence in each class. When a teacher is absent, the prefect notes the absence on the daily report. The school principal is then required to copy this information to a teacher record that includes the reason for the absence. These records are then transferred to the Directorate General of Culture and Education of the Provinces of Buenos Aires, which oversees education matters for the province. Researchers used the daily reports to calculate the class hours missed each day then cross-checked the records against the teacher records to find the reasons for absence, the number of weekly hours worked by a teacher in the school, and whether the absence was reported to the directorate.

17. In each school analysts interviewed the principal and the prefect—a full-time monitoring and disciplinary official who monitors behavioral issues and student and teacher absenteeism. Interviews provided understanding of a typical school day to complement the quantitative data and addressed additional topics, including strategies to recover lost class time, the lag between the beginning of the school year and when all the teaching positions are filled, and the school day schedule when some teaching positions were vacant.

18. Schools do not directly hire official substitute teachers; they are employed and assigned by the province.

19. Questions allowed for multiple responses. The figures given refer to the percentage of total responses, not the percentage of total missed class hours.

20. Schools that serve as polling places often close for cleaning.

21. Muthama and others 2008.

22. See Kenya, Ministry of Health (2004) for evidence.

23. In the following results information on those who were "absent all day" was provided by interviews with administrative staff.

24. Analysts used a logit regression to check for the correlation between employee traits and the number of hours they reported having been absent during the past three months. Because the dependent variable is based on recall and is self-reported, it is not as accurate a measure of absenteeism as the data analysts used in the previous section.

25. Cuevas and Lavarreda 2008.

26. The Department of Guatemala's 715 public primary schools are in both urban and rural settings. Analysts selected 41 using probability proportionate to size sampling based on school size. The sample was stratified by urban or rural location.

27. Some 49 percent of head teachers reported having insufficient funds to purchase supplies in 2007, but head teachers were asked in 2008 to remember the sufficiency of funding in 2007, so these numbers may be less accurate than those for 2008.

28. The discrepancies could also signal other problems, including corruption. For example, analysts found that teaching kits were found to be worth roughly 15 percent less than shown on invoices, which could indicate poor bookkeeping, lax procurement, or room left for side payments.

29. Researchers learned this early on when they had difficulty conducting a pilot study in February 2008 because so few schools had received the first quarterly disbursement of resources.

30. Schools receive milk if they are classified as having high vulnerability to food insecurity or malnutrition. In the Department of Guatemala about a quarter students should be receiving milk; across the country 104 of 333 municipalities have schools that should be receiving milk.

31. However, 21 percent claimed to be left hungry after finishing their meals—and, perhaps related, 28 percent said they shared their meals with siblings.

32. Malinowska-Misiag, Misiag, and Tomalak 2007, 2008.

33. All involved learned from this incident that if service delivery units provide regular detailed financial reports, Public Expenditure Tracking Surveys could be performed regularly at low cost and with large samples to monitor performance.

Recommend solutions

Discerning problems is one thing. Solving them is quite another. Take an example from the previous chapter: analysts found that almost half the teachers in three Ghanaian school districts miss at least a day of school. But are those analysts in a position to develop a solution? Can they figure out what reforms will keep schools open and teachers teaching? And if so, can they convince the government to adopt them? Similar questions could be asked about each of the wide range of problems with the funding and provision of education and health services in developing countries presented in this book. Can independent monitoring organizations determine how supply and staff shortages could be lessened? How budgeting could be made more transparent? How local governments could realize more fully the opportunities that come from decentralizing healthcare or education?

This chapter discusses independent monitoring organizations' approaches to these "how" questions. The examples show that independent monitoring organizations can indeed use their analyses to develop ways to improve service delivery. Their skill at—and their vested interest in—delving deeply into the root causes of service delivery problems often help them develop manageable solutions to those problems. Many of the problems considered in this book seem simple to solve, but that simplicity is often deceptive. Take absenteeism. A knee-jerk reaction to discovering that teachers are being paid for classes that they are not teaching might be to stop paying these teachers. But in the Ghanaian example teachers were absent in part because they have to take long weekday trips to pick up their paychecks or to attend training workshops. In that case, rather than punishing teachers for missing class, the government might try paying teachers and scheduling workshops in ways that do not interfere with teaching. These steps may not solve the whole problem, but they may help, and they may do so simply and inexpensively.

The four organizations in this chapter show that independent monitoring organizations often excel at developing such options. Their analysts are intimately familiar with the local context, with the forces responsible for the status quo, and with how those forces might be changed. And their work is directed at local providers or users of the service. There is a good chance that the analysts' friends or families, or even the analysts themselves, are among the users of a service. This closeness helps them focus on practical steps that lead to short-term, tangible improvements.

Center for Democratic Development, Ghana

Two sets of recommendations in this chapter illustrate the ability of independent monitoring organizations to use their nuanced understanding of a problem to develop workable solutions. The first comes from Ghana, where almost half the teachers in three Ghanaian school districts missed at least one day of teaching during the week analysts from the Center for Democratic Development (CDD) visited schools (see chapter 4).[1] CDD dug deeper into the causes of these absences and found that teachers miss class primarily because of illness, salary collection, funerals, and long-distance lectures. They appear to be less likely to miss class where there is an active parent–teacher association.

CDD used these findings to develop suggestions for reducing absenteeism in Ghana's schools. The recommendations would modify the factors correlated with teacher absenteeism and would strengthen supervision.

Modifying the factors correlated with teacher absenteeism

To address likely causes of teacher absenteeism, CDD made several recommendations, among them:

- Education authorities should adjust the schedule for long-distance education programs so that they do not require teachers to miss class on Fridays. While encouraging teachers to pursue higher education is laudable, the current schedule harms education quality by forcing teachers to skip school to travel to the lectures.
- Teachers should be paid at or near schools so that they do not have to travel to banks in district or regional capitals to collect their paychecks. The recently introduced electronic payment system in Ghana, the "e-zwich," could improve the situation. Some teachers also suggested paying salaries on Saturdays, when teachers are not at work.

Strengthening supervision

To address the part of teacher absenteeism that is due to teachers simply deciding not to show up for work, CDD offered several more recommendations, among them:

- Education officials should actively encourage parent–teacher associations in every school. CDD's study showed that an active parent–teacher association is correlated with higher teacher attendance. They are also less costly than visits by circuit supervisors.
- An evaluation and licensing mechanism should be implemented for teachers and tied to their salaries. Licenses would be renewable based on performance and commitment to the job. CDD discovered during interviews that over the past year 87 percent of teachers had not been sanctioned for absence through salary suspension or even verbal warnings. Teachers themselves might support this policy: 63 percent of teachers interviewed agreed that absent teachers should not be paid for the classes they miss.[2]
- Education officials should discourage local or informal school closures, especially in rural schools. The analysts found instances where school authorities or community members closed down schools without an official reason—particularly because of funerals or so that teachers and students could go to the market.

Centro de Implementación de Políticas Públicas Para el Equidad y el Crecimiento, Argentina

The Center for the Implementation of Public Policies Promoting Equity and Growth (Centro de Implementación de Políticas Públicas Para el Equidad y el Crecimiento, CIPPEC), discussed in chapter 4, found that in two districts in the Province of Buenos Aires, Argentina, the average high school lost five and a half days of class per month, and these losses disproportionately affected poorer schools.[3] CIPPEC's goal was to reduce the loss of scarce education resources and class time due to teacher absenteeism and school closures. To that end, its analysts developed several recommendations for alleviating the factors identified as causing absenteeism and school closures: strikes, heavy workloads, abuses of sick leave, and illness. Because education is already Buenos Aires Province's biggest expense, analysts shied away from recommending new spending to deal with these problems. They tried instead to develop solutions that would help the government more effectively translate education investments into classroom time, which yielded nine recommendations in four categories. The list makes clear CIPPEC's sensitivity to the preoccupations of the various parties and the need for them to accept any recommendations.

Addressing labor inefficiencies and conflicts

- School administrators should build more trusting relationships with teacher unions in order to reach viable agreements more quickly and thereby shorten strikes. Persistent labor conflicts are one of the main obstacles to providing the number of class hours required by the law.
- School labor structures should be modified by hiring teachers in full- or half-time positions rather than on an hourly basis. Currently, many teachers teach at multiple schools in the same year. Exhaustion from constant travel and a heavy workload is a common cause of absenteeism. This new hiring structure would also have the side benefit of making it easier for schools to develop cohesive institutional goals.

Providing teacher assistance

- A teacher health program should be created in alliance with the provincial Ministry of Health, the province, the unions, and teacher health insurance organizations to provide teachers with information on preventing common illnesses and reducing physical and emotional strain from their jobs.
- Teacher training programs and provincial publications and seminars should be modified to cover effective class time and school day organization.
- A support network for teachers who work in schools with more vulnerable or at-risk students should be created to provide professional assistance in working with the student population.

Improving schools

- School infrastructure should be improved. A suitable maintenance policy could help avoid the closures caused by problems with school buildings and reduce repair expenses. Such a policy could include allocating 2–4 percent of the initial cost of school construction to maintenance each year and creating an online registry of complaints about schools and the provincial government's response to allow greater public oversight.

Improving recordkeeping

- Schools should computerize records to track the number of hours and the positions that each teacher works. The lack of cross-checks allows teachers to work a greater number of hours than legally allowed, and teachers' double-booking contributes to absenteeism.
- Schools should create an effective system to monitor and control medical leave. For example, the government could require that medical leave be

granted exclusively by doctors who work for the Directorate General of Culture and Education of the Province of Buenos Aires, with strong sanctions for system abuse.

- The government should periodically monitor effective class hours to assess the impact of these solutions—perhaps designing a survey to evaluate the policies independent of the school administration, so as not to generate incentives to provide false information.

Societatea Academica din Romania, Romania

The third set of recommendations is from the Romanian Academic Society (Societatea Academica din Romania, SAR), an independent monitoring organization whose work is not discussed in earlier chapters. SAR's study examined a pilot education decentralization program, which the Romanian government hoped would improve the education system's responsiveness to local needs.[4] SAR analysts examined the results of the program in 32 pilot schools in four of the eight pilot counties.[5] They found that school budgets are set much as before: rather than being based on decentralized decisionmaking that accounts for contextual factors and specific school needs, school budgets tend simply to mirror budgets from previous years. This system of resource allocation preserves an unfair distribution of funding.[6]

To improve the situation, SAR considered what should be done under three scenarios: improving the status quo, where spending is inert; full decentralization; and SAR's ideal scenario, in which spending is linked with education quality.

Scenario 1: the status quo

Even without decentralizing spending, the status quo has problems, particularly with the organization of education institutions and the transparency of education budgeting. To improve information and transparency about education, SAR recommends that the government establish a new agency to collect and monitor all relevant data on pre-university education. These data should allow the government to better document funding flaws, judge the impact of current programs and arrangements, and foresee changes in demography and the economic health of communities that are likely to affect the local demand for education.

Beyond transparency, SAR suggests several improvements to the institutional structure of Romanian education.

- The Ministry of Education, not the Ministry of Finance, should be fully in charge of the education budget (which by law is set at 6 percent of GDP).
- School principals should be given more responsibility over and training in budgeting and school financial management so that they have the

motivation and ability to improve the effectiveness and efficiency of spending in their schools.

- Key stakeholders—particularly teachers, students, and community representatives—should be involved in decisionmaking. This will help prevent principals from being in full control of budget planning and execution, and together with increased authority of principals will help schools govern themselves more effectively.

Scenario 2: decentralization

If Romania eventually fully decentralizes education financing, SAR offered a number of additional recommendations intended to improve the effectiveness of budgeting.

- A workable per capita allocation formula should be created that bases allocations on the number of students attending schools but that differentiates funding as needed—accounting for such factors as school location and demographics.
- Based on this formula, resources should be allocated directly to local governments, with no intermediary.
- To ensure transparency and accountability, local governments should publicize how they are using their funds.
- Extensive training on the new formula should be provided, particularly for teachers with a negative attitude toward the current pilot decentralization program.

Scenario 3: financing quality

Under SAR's ideal scenario funding would be allocated not only by enrollment but also by education performance, so that money is spent on what works. Though only an ideal, SAR analysts did consider what realizing this scenario would entail. They concluded that the most important requirement would be data. Linking spending and performance would be possible only with robust data on performance, which do not now exist. Thus the government would need a transparent and accessible system of indicators to measure school performance. SAR interviews found teachers and school administrators to be particularly concerned that any such indicators account for the conditions in which the schools operate; thus the government should also gather data on teacher qualifications, school dropouts, failures, truancies, irregular class schedules, and staff absenteeism—as well as on measures taken to address these problems—and incentivize local authorities to accurately record and report the data. With these indicators, government will be able to set quality standards, for schools and teachers, and link them to needed spending—something it now lacks the information to do.

Indo-Dutch Project Management Society, India

The final recommendations in this chapter are from another independent monitoring organization whose study has not yet been considered in this book. The Indo-Dutch Project Management Society (IDPMS) investigated public health centers in the Indian state of Karnataka.[7] Public health centers are supposed to be the first point of contact for rural citizens for government health services, but IDPMS analysts uncovered crippling problems with them. Centers are chronically understaffed and lack adequate infrastructure and even standard pharmaceuticals. The problems undermine care so much that many Karnatakan citizens, even the very poor, prefer to pay for private care instead of using public health centers.

IDPMS found that the Karnataka and federal governments are aware of these problems and in some cases have even made attempts to remedy them. For example, the federal government started the National Rural Health Mission program to reduce the institutional deficiencies in healthcare institutions. But IDPMS's findings suggest that the quality of rural healthcare remains very poor. Analysts thus developed several other steps for both government and nongovernmental organizations to improve rural healthcare.

Analysts focused on three areas in clear need of attention. First, public health centers are inadequately funded. They often lack basic pharmaceuticals, and their infrastructure is often very poor, which makes it difficult to attract qualified medical personnel. IDPMS thus recommends increasing the allocation to health and family welfare to 2 percent of the net state domestic product. (IDPMS points out that this percentage is actually at the low end of the 2–3 percent usually recommended.)

Second, medical supplies are in very short supply because of inadequate funding and an unnecessarily long and complex procurement process. To improve procurement and the general operation of public health centers, IDPMS supports public-private partnerships. The government of Karnataka has already invited private organizations and institutions such as medical colleges, private trusts, and nongovernmental organizations to adopt a few public health centers and run their operations. While still in its infancy, the experiment has been successful so far.

Third, public health centers are chronically understaffed, compounded by high rates of absenteeism, which degrades their quality of care. To some extent addressing the first two shortcomings—inadequate funding and inefficient procurement—will help alleviate this problem by making them better places to work. As it is, funding and supply shortages create conditions that deter all but the most dedicated doctors and healthcare workers from volunteering to work in public health centers.[8] But in addition, the state must aggressively promote medical education to ensure more medical professionals are available to staff the centers.

Community participation might encourage greater efficiency and better allocation of available funds. IDPMS thus suggests that data and information on the procurement process be made publicly available, in accessible terms, so that the community can participate and monitor the process. All relevant data on procurement at all levels should be captured, classified, and presented to the public periodically (via repositories but also workshops and other interactive forums). Such transparency would also increase accountability for supply shortages; the current lack of transparency allows the state to provide poor public healthcare without any repercussions.

IDMPS sees a role for three main actors in improving healthcare delivery: users, the rural communities that use public health centers; government, the provider of public health centers; and independent observers, who can use their expertise and institutional capacity to advise users about the delivery and procurement processes and about how they can pressure the government to improve public healthcare service delivery. All three actors should engage in bilateral discussions to understand each other's issues. IDPMS envisions nongovernmental organizations—both local and external—as independent observers, helping citizens make sense of what is happening in healthcare and push for improvements. In particular, IDPMS sees four activities for nongovernmental organizations:

- Studying the healthcare system, particularly budgets and budgetary procedures, and relating them to locale requirements.
- Explaining in accessible terms these findings to the local and state government health committees and other governing bodies.
- Seeking out the local community's views on its needs and attempting to translate them into a budget.
- Presenting the community-based budgets to subcommittees on health and family welfare at the relevant levels of government.

Conclusion

The same local knowledge that helps independent monitoring organizations discern problems with service delivery in their countries also helps them develop workable solutions to those problems. Independent monitoring organization analysts live with the government and its service delivery methods. They probably know users of government services—and may even be users themselves. This closeness gives them a vested interest in developing practical ways to improve service delivery. It also helps them have a nuanced and comprehensive understanding of the problems with service delivery that they uncover, which makes it easier to analyze what would be required to improve service delivery. Indeed, the organizations in this chapter were often able to identify minor reforms that can easily improve service delivery.

But recommending solutions is only half the story of impact. To improve service delivery, independent monitoring organizations must make the public aware of what they have found, elevating their concerns and calls for reform into the public arena and perhaps even advocating directly for the solutions they have developed. Chapter 6 turns to this final step.

Notes

1. Gyimah-Boadi and others 2008.
2. Of the 37 percent who opposed the proposal, almost half disagreed with it very strongly.
3. Rivas, Malajovich, and Mezzadra 2008.
4. Romanian Academic Society 2008.
5. The pilot program began in 2005 in 8 of Romania's 41 counties; the goal is full decentralization by 2010.
6. Analysts found that average per student spending in the sampled schools was €871, but the standard deviation was €251. The pilot decentralization program has not resulted in funding following students; therefore, it is likely that some students will continue to receive significantly more than others. Continuing this approach to budgeting is likely to undermine schools' motivation to attract more students, since schools receive about the same amount of money as the year before no matter how many students they enroll.
7. IDPMS 2008. IDPMS's study was impressively thorough. Researchers randomly selected 15 public health centers in two districts of Karnataka—Chamarajanagar (CR Nagar) and Bellary—and interviewed more than 2,800 patients—2,530 outpatients and 290 inpatients.
8. Salaries are extremely low compared with those in the private sector, and the vacancies themselves contribute by forcing medical professionals to perform a wide range of additional tasks, from filling prescriptions to running lab tests. Adding to the problem is the lack of living quarters for staff. For example, in Bellary's public health centers analysts found that most doctors are not provided with living quarters, while most nurses and pharmacists are; in CR Nagar most staff are not provided living quarters.

Chapter 6

Disseminate and advocate

After discerning the problems with service delivery, and designing feasible solutions to those problems, the final step for independent monitoring organizations is to inform fellow citizens about their findings and persuade policymakers to implement their solutions. Chapters 2–5 have highlighted independent monitoring organizations' ability to develop subtle understandings of problems with service delivery and to recommend useful solutions. This chapter deals with how independent monitoring organizations finally use their findings.

Independent monitoring organizations can use results from their studies in two ways: disseminating their findings and recommendations and directly advocating for those recommendations. Dissemination seeks to influence the government by informing the public about problems with service delivery and creating public pressure for improvements. In disseminating their results, independent monitoring organizations' usually focus on the users and providers of a service. Because independent monitoring organization analysts are also citizens, they often have an intuitive feel for how best to disseminate (and to whom) and can bring together the government officials, journalists, or nongovernment organization representatives most likely to productively use the findings. This intuitive understanding also helps independent monitoring organizations know when to go beyond reports and slideshows to present their results more creatively, in ways that capture local attention.

This chapter presents several examples: a Ghanaian independent monitoring organization that used the media to ask political candidates hard questions and bring their answers to citizens, an Indian independent monitoring organization that produced a video to make public budgeting interesting and accessible to citizens, a Guatemalan organization that designed a pamphlet that presented its main findings to students and parents as an illustrated story, and a Paraguayan organization that described its education budget findings in a poster that schools in its study could put up in classrooms. These materials are appropriate and accessible to local citizens—written in the local vernacular and consistent with local norms and customs.

This chapter also describes organizations in Poland and Albania that successfully disseminated their findings in more traditional ways—to the media and other civil society groups. In both cases the independent monitoring organizations' local prestige and extensive network of contacts allowed them to bring a tremendous amount of public attention to their findings.

Beyond simply disseminating findings, independent monitoring organizations can be more ambitious and directly advocate for service delivery improvements—and they do not have to do so by themselves. They can exert pressure through the media or get other civil society organizations on board to create broader pressure for change. But sometimes independent monitoring organizations go directly to the government—for example, when they believe their recommendations will be politically beneficial to the government. This chapter discusses a Guatemalan organization that found the government receptive to suggestions for fixing problems in the country's otherwise successful and popular schooling programs. In other cases organizations can build collaborative relationships between analysts and government officials; several organizations sponsored by the Transparency and Accountability Project even involved government officials in their projects from the start. This helped the government view the findings as assets rather than threats, learn about previously unknown problems, and launch reforms or public inquiries.

The results are impressive. At the time of writing, the organizations sponsored by the Transparency and Accountability Project had had only a few months to make their marks on public discourse and policy. By the time this book goes to print, their ongoing work will likely have led to much more. Caution must be used when gauging independent monitoring organizations' effects on public policy. The real effects may not be known for years. And the work documented in this book is often only the beginning: many problems have to be discovered, then rediscovered, and rediscovered again and again before something is finally done about them. Yet despite these caveats, the independent monitoring organizations highlighted here have shown extraordinary potential for bringing about real improvements in service delivery in a remarkably short amount of time.

Center for Democratic Development, Ghana

The Center for Democratic Development's (CDD) analysis of teacher absenteeism in Ghana provided compelling evidence of several diverse factors contributing to teacher absenteeism (see chapter 4), including several that invite relatively simple remedies (see chapter 5).[1] CDD released its report in July 2008 using a strategy carefully calculated to draw public and media attention. It organized a series of media encounters with participants from Parliament, the Ministry of Education, the Ghana Education Service (which employs and supervises teachers), the Ministry of Finance and Economic Planning, the United Nations Children's Fund, the Ghana National Association of Teachers, the Ghana National Association of Graduate Teachers, and other civil society organizations working in education. CDD researchers also participated in live radio discussion programs with the directors of basic education and female education as well as with officials from the Ghana National Education Campaign Coalition.

The strategy worked. The media's reaction was enthusiastic, and six newspapers published major stories. CDD created a media guide for journalists to engage politicians and policymakers on the issues in the run-up to the December 2008 presidential and parliamentary elections.

CDD has already seen some impact from its dissemination. In response to the finding that distance teacher education programs caused absenteeism, the director of basic education at the Ghana Education Service initiated discussions with the universities that conduct the programs to make them less disruptive.

In addition to media outreach, CDD developed a questionnaire on absenteeism for presidential and parliamentary candidates to get them to commit to concrete programs for reducing teacher absenteeism. The questionnaires were used extensively during parliamentary candidate debate forums, which CDD organized in 25 constituencies. CDD also published the report as a research paper and distributed it to key government and education stakeholders and to civil society organizations that advocate for education improvements in Ghana.

El Centro de Investigaciones Económicas Nacionales, Guatemala

Guatemala's National Center for Economic Research (Centro de Investigaciones Económicas Nacionales, CIEN) studied several government programs that provide poor students with scholarships, textbooks, supplies, and meals and milk, and provide teachers with teaching kits (see chapter 4).[2] CIEN found that these programs are fairly effective and that beneficiaries are generally satisfied with them. But it also found that the programs' effectiveness is undermined by delays. Funding and resources arrive long after they should—often many months after the school year has started.

Because CIEN found ways to make popular programs work even better, the Guatemalan government was receptive to its conclusions and has already taken several steps to improve the timeliness of funding. CIEN presented its preliminary results to midlevel officials at the Ministry of Education, and by early October 2008 had arranged to brief Minister of Education Ana Ordóñez de Molina. She in turn served as a panelist at the formal release of the study in late October and announced that the ministry would create rotating funds so that school boards received their first tranche of resources for school meals in December.[3] In December the ministry shifted the start of the school year from mid-January, a starting date rooted mostly in tradition, to February, exactly what CIEN recommended.[4] Because Guatemala's fiscal year begins on January 1, delaying the start of school allows more time to get funds and other resources flowing—though it will probably not solve the problem entirely, as CIEN's data suggest resources in the previous year were not flowing until well into May.

These measurable impacts of CIEN's study are impressive enough. But CIEN also developed a creative and aggressive outreach campaign, including an illustrated pamphlet targeting students, parents, and teachers that presented the main study findings as a story. The pamphlet was released alongside the main report in late October, an event covered by more than 30 journalists, including representatives from five television stations, eight radio stations, and four newspapers and magazines. Articles on the report appeared shortly afterward in several major media outlets.[5] The Ministry of Education is also using CIEN's pamphlet in training sessions for school councils.

Centre for Budget and Policy Studies, India

The Centre for Budget and Policy Studies (CBPS) in the Indian state of Karnataka is also notable for its innovative dissemination strategies.[6] Because district governments in Karnataka receive all their funding as transfers from the state government, they tell the state government what they need each year. In theory, the state's transfers should reflect local needs. But CBPS found that budgeting for health and education spending was entirely top-down. The process of local governments passing expenditure estimates to higher levels is a mere formality; the estimates are generally ignored by the district government and rarely consulted in state-level budget decisions. In the end, the state has little information on local problems or past experiences by the district government of what did and did not work. Because there is little room for information on local needs to travel up the institutional structure and influence budget decisions, budgeting rarely reflects local needs.[7]

Dissemination to government, civil society, and the general public

CBPS's dissemination of its results was wide-ranging and creative. Its most innovative method was a film about its findings and the general budgeting process in Karnataka. The film helped clarify many citizens' hazy ideas about how budgeting works and where in the process to advocate for their agendas. Widely praised, the film is online[8] and was screened several times for grassroots organizations in health and education. One major organization working in primary education reported that the film would help them prepare strategies at the local level.

CBPS also used more traditional dissemination techniques, including a seminar for other civil society organizations that monitor government finance as well as for state government officials and members of district governments. Senior civil servants from the government of Karnataka and the vice president of the government of Chitradurga district attended the January 2008 seminar, which included a 45 minute presentation of the study's findings and an open discussion. CBPS reported that many in the audience had further questions about the functioning of the government and were surprised by and interested in the problems highlighted in the study. For a topic that CBPS acknowledges is not "glamorous," the discussion grew heated and participants animated. The seminar left CBPS optimistic about its dissemination efforts, and the organization plans to host more workshops and events.

The seminar also led to several important moves by the state government. The principal secretary of the Department of Rural Development and the Raj District in the Karnataka government immediately scheduled similar district seminars. After reading the report, the state's principal secretary of finance requested a meeting with officials from various government departments, especially the Finance and Planning Departments, to discuss the findings with CBPS. The secretary remarked that the issues raised by the report are extremely important and "require serious consideration by those deciding on expenditure priorities in Government."[9]

Dissemination in Udupi, one of the two study districts

CBPS involved local decisionmakers in its study from the start and followed up with them as part of its dissemination. In Udupi, one of the two districts investigated, CBPS presented its findings to a small group of elected members of the district government in a workshop. The analysts asked the members how budgeting worked and what the major challenges to improvement were. In general, the feedback corroborated the findings of the formal analysis, including that little information about the district's needs makes it to the state level. The meeting also provided new insights. Participants reported that the district government's expenditure estimates, which it reports to the state government, are usually developed once the district knows how much funding it will receive from the state—that is, once the district knows how much money will be available to it, it plans its own spending for the year; "demand" does not even enter into the picture. Participants also suggested additional problems: for example, funding for health and education is not always completely spent because it does not get to the district government in time. Perhaps most promising, the district government members expressed enthusiasm for the information CBPS uncovered and asked for access to such information on an ongoing basis. They agreed that expenditure records would be helpful in better estimating demand, making expenditure plans each year, and monitoring progress.

Centro de Análisis y Difusión de la Economia Paraguaya, Paraguay

The Center for Analysis and Diffusion of the Paraguayan Economy (Centro de Análisis y Difusión de la Economia Paraguaya, CADEP) wanted to evaluate education spending on 30 primary schools around Asunción, the Paraguayan capital, and found that monitoring the effectiveness of education spending is nearly impossible.[10] More than a decade after major reforms to Paraguay's education system as part of democratization, the country's budgeting for education remains opaque.[11]

CADEP's study has already generated considerable interest from both school officials and parents. To make the findings more accessible, CADEP developed a poster—provided to each classroom in all the study schools—and follow-up seminars on budget management. The seminars are CADEP's second response to the widespread interest in its study: CADEP has fielded requests from schools for seminars on budget management, budget traceability, transparency in schools, and the like.

Beyond dissemination, CADEP has led the construction of a new network of school principals, parent–teacher organizations, nongovernmental organizations, and officials from the Ministry of Education to build a participatory action model for change by communicating and creating interest and awareness, developing managerial and budgeting skills as a group, helping participating schools improve their use of resources, and ultimately improving the quality of education. CADEP has also teamed with two nongovernmental organizations for a much larger two-year study to increase awareness of the importance of monitoring public expenditures and strengthening civil society's ability to participate in budgeting and hold government accountable. CADEP is currently seeking funding for this extension of its work.

In the months ahead, CADEP's general goal is to raise public awareness of the lack of transparency in budgeting and to build support for reforms to the budgeting

process. CADEP held a meeting in early August 2009 with the outgoing vice minister of education as well as a few new officials and scheduled a one-day seminar for
nongovernmental organizations, principals, teachers, supervisors, and Ministry of
Education officials. Speakers included budget specialists and the vice minister of
education. CADEP plans to highlight three themes from its work.

- The need for transparency in all aspects of education management, from
  the Ministry of Education to schools.
- The importance of a traceable budget and management and budget skills
  for school principals.
- The benefits of empowering and supporting parent associations.

Gdansk Institute of Market Economics, Poland

This chapter's final two independent monitoring organizations had simple goals.
Having discovered key features of health and education budgeting that were not
well known in their countries, both tried to inform their fellow citizens—and both
succeeded in achieving high visibility for their studies among the general population and the government.

The first, the Gdansk Institute of Market Economics (GIME) in Poland, conducted two studies as part of the Transparency and Accountability Project. The
studies concluded that Polish hospitals are drowning in debt and that education
financing is inflexible, preserves inequities, and fails to provide clear guidance for
local government spending over and above national subsidies (see chapter 4).[12]
GIME carefully planned its dissemination and appears to have had success: its conclusions about both education and healthcare financing are widely known among
those interested in the two subjects. The project and its results also received a great
deal of media attention in the months after dissemination.

Dissemination of the report on healthcare and education financing

GIME disseminated its first report through a workshop and accompanying press
conference. It also circulated printed copies and summaries of the report—in both
Polish and English—and published a summary article of the report in the *Public Finance Bulletin*, GIME's quarterly publication.[13] An electronic version of the
report and a press release about the study are available on GIME's website.[14]

The February 2008 workshop was hosted jointly with the Ministry of Regional
Development and attended by more than 60 people, including representatives from
national ministries to departments of local self-governments.[15] The animated discussion allowed GIME to establish relations with representatives from the Ministry of
Education, which invited GIME to a separate meeting on education system reform.

GIME also held a press conference in conjunction with the workshop, which about 30 journalists from Reuters, the Polish Press Agency, three newspapers, two magazines, two radio stations, and one television station attended. Participants seemed most interested in education and healthcare service quality and hospital debts, though the discussion also covered healthcare privatization and education subsidies. Most media coverage was articles introducing public finance problems very broadly, though there were exceptions.[16] For example, GIME's recommendations were published in an article in *The Pulse of Medicine* entitled "Basic Health Care Should Be Financed by the Self-Government."

Dissemination of the report on hospital debt

GIME disseminated its second report similarly: with a workshop and press conference and by making the report widely available in print and online.[17]

The September 2008 press conference at the Polish Press Agency was attended by about 35 journalists, including representatives from the Polish Press Agency, major newspapers, weekly news magazines, radio stations, television stations, and specialty magazines, as well as representatives from the Ministry of Health. The first coverage appeared as soon as three hours later and was followed by several radio reports and newspaper articles and an extended interview on TV Biznes, which included comments by the minister of health.

The workshop, held four days after the press conference, was attended by about 15 people, including representatives from the Ministry of Health and the Supreme Control Chamber as well as the director of the Central Health Care Information System, the director of the Voivodship Hospital in Opole, and several representatives of self-government units—including the Marshal's Office of the Opolskie Voivodship, and Warszawa City Hall. GIME analysts included a summary of the discussion in the Polish version of their report, published in late 2008.

GIME's timing in releasing its two reports could hardly have been better. That same fall, the government submitted a bill to parliament to liquidate all public hospitals and have them emerge the following day as shareholder-owned businesses, governed by the same commercial code as other private businesses. Regional and local governments would own the shares, but the facilities would be treated as private businesses under the law. After a vigorous debate, the law was passed by parliament but was vetoed by the president, who is of a different party than the ruling coalition. In February 2009, undaunted, the Council of Ministers passed a resolution to implement the program with incentives for hospitals to participate voluntarily. This "corporatization" program was launched in May 2009. A commitment for adequate funding to implement the program during the economic crisis was agreed between Poland and the World Bank as part of a loan approved in June 2009.

The corporatization plan was almost perfectly in sync with GIME's recommendations. Its purpose was to make hospital managers fully accountable for debts. Hospitals that fail can be put into receivership, reorganized, or closed down. Each hospital participating in the program must have a five-year business plan that will be monitored twice a year by Poland's development bank, the Ministry of Health, the National Health Insurance Fund, and the hospital's owners. These were all core recommendations in GIME's two studies. In addition, GIME's second study offered careful and convincing case studies of four hospitals following four different paths of reform to solve their debt problems (see chapter 4). One of these was corporatized several years ago and is almost an exact template for the approach the current government has chosen. Though conclusively proving GIME's influence is difficult, because reform proposals often have many sources, it is hard to miss the overlap: GIME's work focused on exactly the problem that the government chose to grapple with in the health sector at just the right time, and the government's reform featured the core reform principles GIME suggested.

2A Consortium, Albania

The goal of the final independent monitoring organization discussed in this chapter, 2A Consortium—a partnership between the Albania Center for Economic Research and the Albanian Socio-Economic Think Tank—was also simply to disseminate its findings about budgeting for Albanian healthcare.[18] Albanians know distressingly little about how healthcare budget and spending decisions are made. Data on Albanian healthcare are scarce and frequently suspect,[19] and decision-making power is in the hands of a few experts and a small group of politicians in the central government. There is little to no information on how Albania's healthcare budget is spent.[20] In view of this information deficit, the 2A Consortium set out to draw information about healthcare decisionmaking into the public domain, with the hope that an informed Albanian society would hold its government accountable for healthcare spending and press for more detailed work on budget and spending effectiveness.

2A analysts put a great deal of effort into disseminating their findings. They sought and received wide media coverage of their report, including seven detailed articles in major newspapers and an interview on Tirana National Public Radio. Project staff are now working on a television program for a major channel in Albania, which will cover the motivation for the project, the survey used, and the results and major findings.

2A has also held five major meetings to disseminate its findings: four with government representatives and one with nongovernment experts with influence on healthcare budgeting (two representatives from nongovernmental organizations and three people from academia). The meetings with government representatives were designed to present the findings to government officials who could do something with them. The meeting with nongovernment experts was designed to present the findings and encourage debate over the major issues. The first meeting was a roundtable discussion at the Ministry of Health with the director and three specialists from the Economic Department; the second was a presentation to the Parliamentary Commission of Health in the Albanian Parliament, where attendees expressed willingness to support legal initiatives to improve the health sector; and the third and fourth were meetings with the current and the former (then-current) ministers of health. The former minister of health agreed to establish a National Health Committee through the Council of Ministers as a consultative unit of the Ministry of Health to address some of the 2A report's concerns—though as yet this has failed to materialize.

Conclusion

The final step in an independent monitoring organization's long process of trying to improve service delivery is to disseminate its findings and advocate for improvements. After testing budget transparency by gathering data, after assessing the flow of funds and resources from the treasury to service providers, after evaluating how those resources are used, and after developing solutions to the problems uncovered along the way, analysts finally have the materials to inform their fellow citizens and to push for service delivery improvements. The independent monitoring organizations in this chapter have approached this step in a variety of ways. For some, the goal was simply to inform fellow citizens about how their government spends their taxes—basic information that every citizen should know, but many do not. Other organizations had more ambitious goals, such as influencing policymakers, organizing civil society, or changing policy.

Whatever their goal, all the organizations demonstrate the cumulative value of local knowledge at every step of the process, from choosing a locally important issue or problem, to working to understand and develop solutions to that problem, and finally to disseminating and advocating for solutions. The organizations highlighted in this chapter were able to get their messages out to the media and government. Some drew on links to other civil society organizations. Several went beyond traditional methods and brought otherwise inaccessible findings to a wide, general audience.

These methods worked. In several cases independent monitoring organizations changed the debate, elevating the concerns raised by their studies into the public arena. And some have already had an impact. In Guatemala CIEN's study was directly responsible for a change in the start date of the school year and for shifts in the funding structure of several important student-retention programs. Because of CDD, the Ghana Education Service is revising its distance training program for teachers to reduce its contribution to absenteeism. In these successes, as throughout this book, the independent monitoring organizations' key advantage was local knowledge.

Notes

1. Gyimah-Boadi and others 2008.

2. Cuevas and Lavarreda 2008.

3. See, for example, Álvarez 2008.

4. Villaseñor 2008.

5. See, for example, Flores 2008; *Prensa Libre* 2008; Unda 2008; Radio Punto 90.5 FM 2008.

6. Rath, Madhusudhan, and Tarase 2007.

7. CBPS examined budgeting by looking closely at two districts at very different levels of development. Udupi is on the coast and is among the richer and more socially progressive districts in Karnataka; Chitradurga is a rural, poor inland district. The 2005 human development index ranks Udupi 3rd and Chitradurga 15th among Karnataka's 27 districts (Karnataka, Planning and Development Department 2006).

8. See www.solutionexchange-un.net.in/decn/cr/res09070810.avi.

9. Letter from R. Sreenivasa Murthy, principal secretary to the Government Finance Department, Government of Karnataka, to Dr. Vinod Vyasulu, director, CBPS, 15 March 2008.

10. Brizuela Speratti 2008.

11. CADEP found that poor transparency pervades the entire budgeting system, from salaries to funds for repairs and supplies. For example, when the Ministry of Education initiated a program to distribute academic kits—notebooks, pencils, an eraser, and a ruler—to students, it could not develop a budget for the program because it did not know how many students would need it. Schools that eventually received the kits did so only after making a special request to the ministry.

12. Malinowska-Misiag, Misiag, and Tomalak 2007, 2008.

13. *Public Finance Bulletin* 25(1).

14. For the report, see www.ibngr.edu.pl/pdf/publikacje/raporty/Centralne_finansowanie. pdf (Polish) or www.ibngr.edu.pl/pdf/publikacje/raporty/Centralized_financing_v2.pdf

(English). For the press release, see www.ibngr.edu.pl/pdf/konferencje/feioz11-02-2008. pdf.

15. "Local self-governments" is the term GIME used for all governments below the national government. Attendees included representatives from many different ministries. Represented departments from the Ministry of Finance included the Regional Policy and Agriculture Department, the Budget Zone Financing Department, the State Budget Department, the Local Government Finances Department, and the Paying Authority Department. Represented departments from the Ministry of Regional Development included the Department of Structural Policy Coordination, the Department of Community Support Framework Coordination and Management, the Information and Publicity Department, and the Department for Aid Programs and Technical Assistance. Several representatives from the Central Statistical Office attended, including both the National Accounts and Finance Statistics Divisions. And representatives from several self-governments attended, including the Marshal's Offices of the Wielkopolska and Silesia Regions and the Marshal's Offices of the Dolnośląskie and Podkarpackie Voivodships. Finally, representatives came from many nongovernmental organizations, including the Warsaw School of Economics, the Center for Social and Economic Research, and the Wroclaw Regional Development Agency.

16. Several journalists also conducted follow-up interviews with GIME researchers, several of which were published. One of the authors also appeared on a television program called "Business Lunch" on TNV TNBS.

17. At the time of writing, only the English version of the report had been disseminated (www.ibngr.edu.pl/pdf/publikacje/raporty/GIME_Final_Report_August_29 .pdf). The press release is available at www.ibngr.edu.pl/pdf/konferencje/Konferencja _22092008_Material.pdf, and the presentation from the press conference is available at www.ibngr.edu.pl/pdf/konferencje/Konferencja_22092008_Prezentacja.pdf.

18. Preci and others 2008.

19. For example, data on life expectancy vary by source. According to government statistics, Albania has the highest life expectancy in the Balkans, while World Health Organization statistics show it as having the lowest.

20. Researchers surveyed administrators and patients in a nationwide sample of 47 healthcare facilities (31 primary healthcare centers, 6 hospitals, and 10 local government units). Almost 60 percent of interviewees reported not knowing the budgeting methodology used in health, and many do not know who approves the final budget. This is no wonder, as record-keeping is poor and auditing negligible. Analysts discovered large discrepancies between the funding transferred by the central government and the funding regional and local government units reported receiving.

Chapter 7

Possibilities and lessons of independent monitoring

This book opened with a simple idea. No one is better placed to judge a government than those it governs, and no one is better positioned to monitor government services to ensure that they perform well and transparently than the citizens who use those services. The embodiment of this idea is the independent monitoring organization—typically a small group of analysts and advocates who assess government policies and services in the hope of improving transparency and performance. Independent monitoring organizations have a head start in assessing the government because their analysts are also citizens. They live with the government. They use its services and pay for them with their taxes. They have a sense of what government services are working well or poorly. Their experience leads them to ask questions and pursue issues that resonate with users. It helps them frame fairly narrow, manageable studies that can identify feasible reforms. It influences how they undertake every step of their investigation. And it provides them with an invaluable personal commitment to producing work that leads to real improvements in government services.

This argument is intuitive. But it is not automatically true. While in theory independent monitoring organizations have an ideal vantage point from which to assess the government, they also face many obstacles. Rigorously assessing government performance is not easy. It requires funding, access to data, skilled analysts, analytical techniques appropriate to the questions being asked, and an interest in using unbiased research to frame solutions to problems. And there is no guarantee that rigorous assessment will lead to real improvements in government performance, a task that requires a new set of skills and understanding, as well as the commitment to developing realistic solutions and convincing decisionmakers and voters to adopt them. Without a clear purpose, time frame, and a little help along the way, the sheer complexity and Sisyphean nature of the enterprise might easily push an independent monitoring organization off track.

This is where a program like the Transparency and Accountability Project can make a difference. It provides funding, structure, a rigorous timeline, a set of techniques and materials on using them, technical help as needed, examples, and—perhaps most important—an opportunity for peer review and the added inducement of friendly competition with like-minded organizations. The long-term effects of this one-time support for the independent monitoring organizations highlighted in this book cannot be known after such a brief pilot intervention. But the initial signs are remarkably promising. Not only did the organizations produce works of impressive quality, but each one would subject itself to the program again. They were unanimously pleased with their own work and with the process of engaging with other organizations doing similar work on the same timeline.

In view of these positive results, this volume closes with a few thoughts on the lessons that can be drawn from the Transparency and Accountability Project.

Lessons about independent monitoring organizations—from each step and the process as a whole

Each step of the independent monitoring organizations' work yields important lessons, as does the process as a whole. This section considers those lessons in detail.

Selecting an analytical topic

The first lesson is the seemingly inherent tendency of independent monitoring organizations to choose specific, manageable topics of local importance—and with a creativity that puts long-established techniques for monitoring governments to a wide range of novel uses. The Transparency and Accountability Project's first request for proposals asked only that the independent monitoring organizations use program budgeting techniques to analyze spending. Even at that level of generality, the responses were remarkably varied and specific to pressing domestic issues. At the time, the Russian Federation was beginning to base its budgets on the performance of the previous year's spending rather than on the previous year's budgets, a shift that the federal government encouraged for regional governments. In this context, one independent monitoring organization asked whether performance-based budgeting could be detected in two Russian regions. In Indonesia, which had recently decentralized health and education financing, an independent monitoring organization proposed testing whether national, provincial, and district governments were meeting obligations, focusing on just three districts. In the Indian state of Karnataka an independent monitoring organization wanted to know whether the state government was realizing its stated commitment to expand funding for health and education and whether funding was aligned with needs of the population. An independent monitoring organization in Ghana proposed a study of whether budgets actually matched spending on education and health. So, from one general question came a rich variety of responses—all based on local issues—and research plans scaled to what each organization could manage.

In later rounds the additional strictures—that independent monitoring organizations use public expenditure tracking and absenteeism instruments to investigate a problem in education or health—were added and led to an explosion of creativity in how these techniques might be applied to local issues. In Kenya, was the Secondary Education Bursary Scheme performing as designed? In Peru, do two highly visible national priority health programs for immunization and tuberculosis prevention function well at the clinic level where the services are delivered? In India, where the failure of public sector primary care services has led to 90 percent of health expenditures coming out of people's pockets, could a joint expenditure and absenteeism study shed light on what to do to turn the situation around?

Now, with this book, this extraordinary range of topics are out in the world for other independent monitoring organizations and civil society organizations to read about, as are the instruments and background materials used by the project to support them. In future grant rounds, and as organizations proceed on their own, these examples[1] will expand the potential for monitoring local service delivery well beyond the traditional measures that professional researchers have used in standard efficiency and equity studies.

Gathering budget data

Access to data was expected to be the single biggest obstacle for organizations participating in this project. And indeed, some organizations struggled mightily to gather needed information. In Kenya, for example, where an independent monitoring organization studied both education and health, analysts had no trouble investigating the secondary school bursary scheme, while the team investigating absenteeism in healthcare was stonewalled until the very last minute they could feasibly have started their fieldwork.

Yet on the whole most groups were able to gain access to the existing data that they needed or had few problems collecting primary data from schools and health providers. When data were initially withheld and obtained only with great effort, the main reason appeared to be incomplete, invented, or just inaccurate data. In fact, accessing data was much easier than using data. In many cases the data were nearly impossible to assemble into program categories, or there were so many funding flows that it was hard to piece together the entire picture. In the end the process of gathering data and turning data into usable information turned out to be of enormous value to the organizations, offering them a sense of whether the government itself knows what it is doing.

Following the money

The independent monitoring organizations excelled at following the money. One organization in Karnataka literally followed funds with a video camera to show other organizations and regular citizens the difference between a competent manager of public funds and an incompetent one. It recorded the difficulties that all local government officials have wresting control from state bureaucrats, even over activities for which they were legally responsible. From Guatemala to Ghana to Albania, it is hard to overstate the impressiveness of the independent monitoring organizations' work in this area—their perseverance in digging through a morass of budgets and institutional channels to trace where money went, through which streams, and delayed by which bottlenecks. Indeed, it is hard to imagine their work being replicated by any other type of organization. The same holds true for the detailed detective work required for the absenteeism studies, including the cross-checking with administrative data and qualitative interviews with stakeholders who observe work patterns daily.

Examining the spending

For independent monitoring organizations analysis is largely descriptive. Their primary role is monitoring, not evaluation. The organizations highlighted in this book tended to succeed in their analysis when they presented carefully collected and disaggregated data simply and directly as part of their key findings. All the organizations were more than capable of handling the analysis, and the presentation of results was often quite clever. The Center for the Implementation of Public Policies Promoting Equity and Growth (Centro de Implementación de Políticas Públicas Para el Equidad y el Crecimiento), for example, used the findings from its absenteeism study to try to quantify absenteeism's cost to schools and then asked whether the lost resources could be recovered. The Centre for Regional Information and Studies (Pusat Telaah dan Informasi Regional), faced with extraordinarily complicated funding streams to schools, showed the complex performance measures of each stream on a single page. Both of the studies by the Gdansk Institute of Market Economics made liberal use of maps and graphs to show key results and illustrated complex issues through a series of tables that followed a similar format (so once readers mastered the first table, they could easily follow the rest). The Center for Budget and Policy Studies presented results in simple tables that unambiguously backed up its surprising finding of falling per capita spending in health and education despite rising state resources in two very different districts. The simplicity made the message loud and clear—and gave no hint of the difficult task the center's analysts faced in disentangling virtually indecipherable budgets to arrive at their conclusion. These are just a few examples of the remarkable range of ways in which the independent monitoring organizations presented findings that average citizens could understand.

Recommending solutions

At the start of this project, concern existed that the independent monitoring organizations would already know what changes they wanted and would recommend them no matter what their analysis showed. This concern was unfounded. In fact, a few exceptions aside, there was remarkable consistency between the independent monitoring organizations' findings and recommendations. For the most part the scope of the studies was limited to something that could be understood quickly, and the recommendations tended to have the same character. Although some independent monitoring organizations were tempted to offer too many proposals, on the whole the recommendations had limited scope and could be implemented quickly and easily; they were things that could have been done yesterday.

Disseminating and advocating—or constructive engagement

Most of this book uses "advocacy" to describe the final step in the process, but "constructive engagement" might better capture the efforts of many of the groups. It is doubtful that any outside agency has much to teach these groups about dissemination and engaging their audiences. But the organizations themselves learned a great deal from each other, exchanging war stories and strategies, often with great humor, during peer review sessions. The independent monitoring organizations sponsored by the Transparency and Accountability Project tend to lack access to the highest levels of national government—though there are exceptions. But all have access to technical levels or to local government leaders. Their primary audience is the public, and they tend to try to influence government through such channels as the press, radio, television, voters, and other advocacy organizations. Most are masters at matching the means and tenor of the message to the audience. And, as noted earlier, language and presence on the ground—which are often barriers for outside agencies—are innate advantages of independent monitoring organizations.

Independent monitoring in general

The project also produced a few more general lessons. The first is the value of local knowledge. "Local" appears many times in this book. If independent monitoring organizations' success is defined as achieving reform, the most successful organizations in this book tailored every aspect of their work—from choosing a question to advocating for solutions—to their local context. Independent monitoring organizations may sometimes face the temptation to emulate the preoccupations and methods of external analysts, but they do so at the risk of abandoning their greatest strengths. Independent monitoring organizations' natural audience is internal, not external, and this is the right audience. Independent monitoring organizations know how to reach the decisionmakers who matter to their issues, even if their methods may seem roundabout.

Second, in achieving reform, careful analysis of the problem makes all the difference. Simply advocating for general improvement, like lower absenteeism of teachers or health workers, may feel right and be an important first step, but it rarely does much to reach that goal. Advocating instead for a reasonable reform to reduce absenteeism—one that is derived from empirical knowledge—has far greater potential to move the agenda forward, even if incrementally.

By contrast, analysis often does little without advocacy. Analysis by itself, put on a shelf in the hope someone else takes it up, can be an important first step. But this book shows that the task of developing feasible recommendations colors the analysis, focusing and disciplining it. An organization that knows it will need to present feasible recommendations openly, and expose those recommendations to criticism, is highly motivated to undertake analysis that focuses on what will actually improve government service.

Finally, the structure and process of the Transparency and Accountability Project works well. The project supports independent monitoring organizations jointly producing small, self-selected analytical tasks, along the same timeline and using similar techniques, and culminating in a joint review of each other's work. The results speak for themselves. Indeed, the process is exhilarating for all involved.

The future of monitoring governments

The 19 projects highlighted in this book show beyond a doubt the effectiveness of independent monitoring organizations in monitoring specific aspects of government performance. The Transparency and Accountability Project is one approach to supporting independent monitoring organizations, with a unique focus on learning by doing. Some external groups provide core support to organizations to help them get on their feet and continue to support their development, sometimes for a long time, until they become at least partially self-sustaining. Other donors provide support for specific projects. Independent monitoring organizations also have access to many types of training, through a variety of outlets. The Transparency and Accountability Project's support, by contrast, was limited, focused by the proposition that the best way to help organizations monitor government expenditures and implementation is to help them follow the five steps reviewed in this book. Learning these steps by doing them together with like-minded organizations in other countries is one way to build independent monitoring organization capacity and effectiveness while reducing the need for outside experts except for specialized needs.

The internal accountability that independent monitoring organizations provide has complementarity with traditional external accountability that is just waiting to be exploited. But exploiting it will require sometimes risky changes in behavior by several parties. International organizations need to realize that partnerships with local organizations can be beneficial to both sides, governments need to encourage such partnerships, and independent monitoring organizations need to feel that they can engage in such partnerships without losing their independence. These requirements may prove onerous. Yet the results in this book provide ample reason for trying.

The Transparency and Accountability Project is a pilot, and the results in this book are only its first. But they show tremendous promise. The project is continuing to fund new independent monitoring organizations, and with persistence it should provide a growing body of evidence, instruments, methods, and examples to similar organizations wanting to improve their governments' spending and service delivery.

Note

1. Materials and reports from the organizations can be downloaded from the Transparency and Accountability Project website (http://tap.resultsfordevelopment.org/resources).

References

Abadzi, Helen. 2007. "Absenteeism and Beyond: Instruction Time Loss and Consequences." Policy Research Working Paper 4376. World Bank, Washington, DC.

Adamtey, Nicholas, Bishop Akolgo, Nii Moi Thompson, Ama Blankson Anaman, Gladys Ohene Darko, Daniel Chachu, Sylvester Bagooro, and Luke Atazona. 2007. "Policy Analysis and Review of Trends in Public Spending for Education and Health in Ghana in the Last Five Years (2002–2006)." Integrated Social Development Centre, Accra. [http://tap.resultsfordevelopment.org/resources/analysis-trends-public-spending-education-and-health-2002-2006].

Alvarado, Betty, and Eduardo Morón. 2007. "Hacia un Presupuesto por Resultados: Afianzando la Transparencia y Rendición de Cuentas." Centro de Investigación de la Universidad del Pacífico, Lima. [http://tap.resultsfordevelopment.org/resources/towards-results-based-budget].

———. 2008. "The Route of Expenditures and Decision Making in the Health Sector in Peru." Centro de Investigación de la Universidad del Pacífico, Lima. [http://tap.resultsfordevelopment.org/resources/route-expenditure-and-decision-making-health-sector].

Álvarez, Alejandra. 2008. "Clases podrían dar inicio el 1 de febrero." October 20. *Pensa Libre*. [www.prensalibre.com/pl/2008/octubre/20/270345.html].

Brizuela Speratti, Cynthia. 2008. "Education Expenditures: Budget Tracking Analysis of Thirty Paraguayan Educational Institutions." Centro de Análisis y Difusión de la Economía Paraguaya, Asunción. [http://tap.resultsfordevelopment.org/resources/education-expenditures-budget-tracking-analysis-thirty-paraguayan-educational-institutions].

Cuevas, Mario, and Jorge Lavarreda. 2008. "Expenditure Tracking to Improve the Effectiveness of Public Education in Guatemala." Centro de Investigaciones Económicas

Nacionales, Guatemala. [http://tap.resultsfordevelopment.org/resources/expenditure-tracking -improve-effectiveness-public-education-guatemala].

De Ferranti, David, Anthony J. Ody, Justin Jacinto, and Graeme Ramshaw. 2009. *How To Improve Governance.* Washington, DC: Brookings Institution Press.

Dirección General de Cultura y Educación. 2007. Cobertura del Sistema Educativo y Pobreza. Serie Información Estadística. Dirección de Información y Estadística, La Plata.

Flores, Ligia. 2008. "Fallas en ejecución educativa." La Hora, October 27. [www.lahora.com.gt/ notas.php?key=38822&fch=2008%E2%80%9010%E2%80%9027].

Freedom House. 2008. *Freedom in the World.* Washington, DC: Freedom House.

Ghana, Ministry of Finance. 2008. "Budget Statement." Government of Ghana, Accra.

Griffin, Charles. 2009. "Reducing Corruption in the Health and Education Sectors." In Robert I. Rotberg, ed., *Corruption, Global Security, and World Order.* Washington, DC: Brookings Institution Press.

Griffin, Charles, David de Ferranti, Chinyere Bun, Justin Jacinto, Graeme Ramshaw, and Courtney Tolmie. 2009. *Lives in the Balance: Improving Accountability for Public Spending in Developing Nations.* Washington, DC: Brookings Institution Press.

Grindle, Merilee Serrill. 2007. *Going Local: Decentralization, Democratization, and the Promise of Good Governance.* Princeton, NJ: Princeton University Press.

Gyimah-Boadi, E., Joseph Asunka, George Ofosu, and Daniel Armah-Attoh. 2008. "Tracking Leakage of Public Resource in Education." Center for Democratic Development, Accra. [http://tap.resultsfordevelopment.org/resources/tracking-absentee-rates-among-primary -school-teachers-ghana].

IDPMS (Indo-Dutch Project Management Society). 2008. "Following the Public Health Delivery Trail." Indo-Dutch Project Management Society, Bangalore. [http://tap.resultsfordevelopment. org/resources/following-health-delivery-trail].

INDEC (Instituto Nacional de Estadística y Censos de la Republica Argentina). 1984. "La Pobreza en la Argentina." Series Study 1. Instituto Nacional de Estadística y Censos de la República Argentina, Buenos Aires.

Institute for Urban Economics. 2007. "Public Health and Education Expenditures Analysis in the Russian Federation in 2004–2006." Institute for Urban Economics, Moscow. [http:// tap.resultsfordevelopment.org/resources/budget-expenditures-education-and-healthcare -russia-2004-2007].

Karnataka, Planning and Statistics Department. 2006. *Karnataka Human Development Report 2005.* Karnataka, India: Government of Karnataka.

Kenya, Ministry of Health. 2004. "Human Resource Mapping and Verification Exercise." Government of Kenya, Nairobi.

Kibua, Thomas, Lineth N. Oyugi, Andrew Riechi, and Evelyn Anupi. 2008. "Expenditure Tracking of Secondary Education Bursary Scheme in Nairobi Province, Kenya." Institute of Policy

Analysis and Research, Nairobi. [http://tap.resultsfordevelopment.org/resources/expenditure-tracking-secondary-education-bursary-scheme-kenya].

Malinowska-Misiag, Elzbieta, Wojciech Misiag, and Marcin Tomalak. 2007. "Poland Centralized Financing of the Health Care and Education." Gdansk Institute for Market Economics, Gdansk. [http://tap.resultsfordevelopment.org/resources/centralized-financing-healthcare-and-education].

————. 2008. "The Use of Public Resources in Hospitals." Gdansk Institute for Market Economics, Gdansk. [http://tap.resultsfordevelopment.org/resources/use-public-resources-hospitals].

Munteanu, Igor, Tatiana Lariushin, Veaceslav Ionita, and Angela Munteanu. 2008. "Decentralisation of the Education Reform and Spending for Education." Institute for Development and Social Initiatives, Chisinau. [http://tap.resultsfordevelopment.org/resources/targeting-education-policy-review-decentralized-public-spending].

Muthama, Thomas Mutinda, Thomas Muchoki Maina, Justus Inonda Mwanje, and Thomas Nzioki Kibua. 2008. "Absenteeism of Health Care Workers in Machakos District, Kenya: Incidence, Determinants and Consequences." Institute of Policy Analysis and Research, Nairobi. [http://tap.resultsfordevelopment.org/resources/evaluation-health-providers-absenteeism-health-sector].

Preci, Zef, Fatmir Memaj, Klodjan Seferaj, Fran Brahimi, Gjovalin Preci, Jollanda Memaj, and Mimoza Kasimati. 2008. "Improving Public Expenditure Effectiveness in Health Sector." 2A Consortium, Tirana. [http://tap.resultsfordevelopment.org/resources/improving-public-expenditure-effectiveness-health-sector].

Prensa Libre. 2008. "Informe evidencia deficiencias en sector educativo." October 27. [www.prensalibre.com/pl/2008/octubre/27/272586.html].

Radio Punto 90.5 FM. 2008. "CIEN informó de atraso de ejecución presupuestaria del MINEDU." October 27, 3:19 p.m. [www.transdoc.com.gt/interna.php?id=7935].

Rath, Sharadini, B.V. Madhusudhan, and Ganapathi Tarase. 2007. "Expenditure on Education and Health at the Local Level." Centre for Budget and Policy Studies, Bangalore. [http://tap.resultsfordevelopment.org/resources/expenditure-health-and-education-two-districts].

Rivas, Axel, Laura Malajovich, and Florencia Mezzadra. 2008. "Equity and Effectiveness of the Public Expenditure in Schools in Argentina." Centro de Implementación de Políticas Publicas Para el Equidad y el Crecimiento, Buenos Aires. [http://tap.resultsfordevelopment.org/resources/equity-and-effectiveness-expenditure-schools-argentina].

Romanian Academic Society. 2008. "Lights and Shadows in the Romanian Schools." Romanian Academic Society, Bucharest. [http://tap.resultsfordevelopment.org/resources/effectiveness-and-efficiency-public-expenditure-romanian-education-system].

Septyandrica, Chitra R. 2008. "Is Education Budget Efficiently Spent?" Pusat Telaah dan Informasi Regional, Jakarta. [http://tap.resultsfordevelopment.org/resources/education-budget-efficiently-spent].

Sumindar, Riyan, Siti Fatimah, Alwin Khafidhoh, Markus Christian, and Suhud Darmawan. 2007. "Public Spending for Education and Health at National, West Java Province, and 3 (three) Municipalities in West Java (Bandung, Sumedang, and Banjar) over the Past Five Years." Bandung Institute of Governance Studies, Bandung. [http://tap.resultsfordevelopment.org/resources/local-innovations-public-spending-management-indonesia].

Toshniwal, Kriti, and Vinod Vyasulu. 2008. "Karnataka: Fiscal Correction for Human Development?" Center for Budget and Policy Studies, Bangalore. [www.cbpsindia.org/files/Symposium-KarnatakaFinances-May2008.pdf].

Unda, Mercedes C. 2008. "CIEN: útiles no llegan a tiempo." *Siglo XXI*, 28 October. [www.sigloxxi.com/noticias/24147].

Villaseñor, Claudia Méndez. 2008. "Clases se inician en febrero." *Prensa Libre*, December 30. [www.prensalibre.com.gt/pl/2008/diciembre/30/285991.html].

Index